Your Spacious Self

Your Spacious Self

Clear Your Clutter and Discover Who You Are

A Journey in Six Stages

Stephanie Bennett Vogt

iUniverse, Inc.
New York Lincoln Shanghai

Your Spacious Self
Clear Your Clutter and Discover Who You Are

iUniverse books may be ordered through booksellers or by contacting:

iUniverse
2021 Pine Lake Road, Suite 100
Lincoln, NE 68512
www.iuniverse.com
1-800-Authors (1-800-288-4677)

Author photo by Daphne Weld Nichols

ISBN: 978-0-595-41868-8 (pbk)
ISBN: 978-0-595-86215-3 (ebk)

Printed in the United States of America

To Jay and Camilla.
I love you more than words can say.

♋

To be born into and inhabit the physical is a miracle.
To be born into, inhabit, and choose to WAKE UP in the physical …
*is **breathtaking**.*

—Stephanie Bennett Vogt

♋

Contents

Part II—The Journey of Clearing

Preface

What you are is what you have been.
What you will be is what you do now.
—The Buddha

What can I say? I'm a teacher. I love to extract the deeper truths from things and convey them in ways that people can understand and use every day. But we all know that life doesn't always lend itself to being tidied or packaged. Our experiences don't always add up at the end of the day. No number of well-crafted summary points can capture the essence of a journey, especially when it comes to clearing our clutter. This is why it's taken me years to write this book.

But if I had to summarize in three words the essence of the clearing path as I've experienced it over the past ten years it would be these: Raise, release, reveal.

I call them my "three R's." Clearing *raises* awareness. Clearing *releases* attachments. Clearing *reveals* a spacious part in us that has been there all along. The three fit together as one organic whole: The more aware we become about the places we hold on, the more likely we are to let them go. The more we let go, the more spacious we feel. The more spacious we feel, the easier it is to clear the next thing or issue. Sound good?

If it were that simple there would be no need for this book. You could stop right now and go "do" clearing. The thing is, clutter has no concept of simple. The clearing path is messy and meandering and full of unexpected surprises. Clearing clutter is not just something we do, like taking a class or going on a diet. It is a journey that is nearly impossible to measure, quantify, or even describe.

But I am a seasoned teacher, after all, and I love a good challenge. With over thirty years of teaching and clearing experience, I believe I have broken the code on this slippery, colorful subject. I'm ready to share what I've learned about the journey and offer a model for clearing that is both radical in its message and elegant in its simplicity; a model that comes field-tested and uses my life as a principal source.

The question is innocent enough. It's asked all the time, right after your name, rank, and serial number. But telling people what I do for a living never fails to raise an eyebrow or two. "Space clearing practitioner" usually draws a quizzical "Come again?" from folks trying to figure out if it's something they can relate to, like clutter clearing, or if it's something weirder than that. Telling people that space clearing[1] is "an intuitive practice that harmonizes the flow of energy in spaces at very deep levels" is likely to turn a blank stare into a glazed stare ... but quickly adding, "It's a cousin of *Feng Shui*," usually brings them back. Saying that I'm a healer of "sick" homes and workplaces, or that I clear "invisible clutter," or that I help people "release stress and lighten their emotional load," might elicit a knowing nod that makes what I do sound almost normal, but still, doesn't quite do it. I'm working on it.

The question I'd really like to answer is *how* I left a successful twenty-year career as a high school Spanish teacher to land in a profession that is mostly unknown and unheard of in the West, though it comes with its own set of challenges. Going from a career that is mainstream and credible to one that is unconventional and intrinsically mysterious, after all, doesn't exactly fit our idea of a natural progression.

I've thought of this idea of progression a lot since I made the switch over ten years ago, and I've come to realize these two occupations have a lot more in common than one might expect. Explaining principles of "non-local mind," or "compassionate non-attachment" to a left-brained client, for example, is not all that different from teaching a foreign language to a high school kid. I'm still creating opportunities for people to experience a world that is different from their own; still looking for safe, practical, and fun applications that stretch and engage and move people beyond their self-concept and comfort zone. The language itself may have changed; so, too, the schoolroom. Besides that, it's not that big a departure. I feel right at home.

How I got into space clearing might sound rather bland after that introduction, but it's something most of us can relate to and it's ... well ... the honest-to-God truth: I was suffocating. Everywhere I looked there was *stuff* ... and all that stuff was slowly squeezing me to death.

Though modest in the beginning, the process of shedding my physical clutter seemed to grow organically—exponentially—gaining momentum with every pass. Searching for a pen in the drawer that was jammed to the gills with every conceivable writing implement (including the pristine box of personalized pencils that I got when I was in grammar school) led to clearing that drawer and the one below it, which led to clearing the entire desk, and the bookcase, and the piles of magazines with the mouth-watering recipes I never got around to trying.

Looking for a plastic food container led to recycling dozens of excess lidless yogurt cups, consolidating the condiments in the fridge, tossing unidentifiable freezer items laden with inches of frost. Removing sticky bulletin board notices, dog-eared flyers, expired coupons, stale artistic masterpieces, and rubbery refrigerator magnets (selling pest management services) led to the long-over-due renovation project that opened up a dividing wall in our kitchen, added a fresh, colorful coat of paint, and offered a new lease on life.

The easy things led to clearing more difficult ones like the clothes I might be able to fit in again someday (not), my daughter's adorable baby clothes, my matchbook collection, all my graduate school term papers, classroom notes, and twenty years of teaching paraphernalia.

The clearing process led to creating soothing, repetitive rituals like sweeping the kitchen floor, unloading the dry dishes to make room for the wet ones, rounding up the family room before going to bed, giving my car keys a permanent home and putting them away every day.

Before I knew it, my clearing efforts grew into something way bigger than a string of random feel-good exercises. It became a journey—a journey that had much less to do with clearing out "things" than it did with clearing out my *attachments* to things.

Weeding out the material excesses of my home and office became an enlightening practice of *feeling* the experience of clearing. Feeling how congested or gummy or even nauseous I can be after an hour of moving junk around. Feeling how much my feet hurt or how clearing makes me more thirsty and sluggish. Feeling how hard and painful and embarrassing it is to let some things go. Feeling how good it feels in the house after I've put stuff in the recycling bin and walked it out to the curb for the Friday morning pick-up. Feeling my feelings fully and completely without attaching any more drama to them or taking them personally.

Clearing has taken other forms as well, like giving myself some slack when I recognize that I've gotten lost in yet another round of self-judgment. I've cleared by breathing deeply instead of binging on the million ways I could have done something better. I've cleared by exercising gentle self-care when I feel too jangled and worn out to care about anything or anyone after a long day.

I've cleared by observing the rising heat level when someone I care about, or don't even know (like the tail-gating maniac), presses my buttons. I've cleared by feeling the intense charge, and discomfort, of a difficult situation instead of trying to fix or stuff the pain. I've cleared by choosing laughter over taking myself too seriously.

I've cleared by teaching others about clearing. I've cleared by writing a book about clearing—several times. I've cleared by taking my over-written, pudgy, manuscript down to the studs and re-building the entire thing when it's the last thing I want to do and can't imagine finding it within myself to dig deeper. I've cleared by allowing this book to take eight years to gestate, to evolve along with me, to be the best that it can possibly be.

I've cleared by being as mindful and aware as possible—one drawer, pile, step, moment, or breath at a time.

That is how I got into this clearing business.

And if people are still with me after listening to my long-winded spiel, I might leave them with this little nugget: I tell them: If you want to be more in the flow and discover what makes your heart sing, you can begin the way I did. Start by clearing out a drawer and *feel* what it feels like. And then do it again. And again. And keep going.

Joseph Campbell probably best captures the moment my life took a radical turn. This simple one-line summary I found on the Internet describes the first step of the Hero's Journey, aptly entitled "Departure":

> "The call to adventure is the point in a person's life when they are first given notice that everything is going to change, whether they know it or not."[2]

My "notice" came almost exactly ten years ago, inelegantly kicked off by a severe case of the flu that was to last the better part of four weeks. What started as a garden-variety sore throat—which I attributed to the stress of holiday season—morphed into a fever, a cough that wouldn't quit, a bad case of insomnia, and, my first-ever sinus infection, which was so painful that I thought I would go mad. The meds that helped relieve the pain in my head would deliver a terrible upset in my stomach. Placing my hand to contain one leak would uncover another. I felt like a ship that was running aground.

Desperate to fix this thing, I grasped at anything I could get my hands on: antibiotics, codeine syrup, homeopathic remedies, teas and tinctures, vitamin pills. I ranted and thrashed and sweated. Nothing was working. I couldn't stand feeling so sick. I couldn't tolerate lying in bed like that, doing *nothing* but hacking my guts out. I couldn't bear not knowing what was happening to me.

My approach to any life challenge at that time had always followed a logical sequence: If something doesn't work, you fix it. You figure it out, you force or will it to change if you have to. You *do* something about it. I had no concept that my body, in its infinite wisdom, knew exactly what it was doing to heal and rebalance itself. Bodies, like homes, are in a constant state of rebalancing all the time, creating and adjusting as they dance with the choices we make and the laws of nature. My job, if I had only chosen to listen, was to get out of the way!

A full-blown body rash seemed like a fitting end to a month of poor-me shenanigans. This last straw was so bad it was funny. And because I could finally laugh about it, I began to let go and (surprise, surprise) … to get well.

In hindsight I can see how my body was simply reflecting back to me the huge build-up of stress that I had not bothered to recognize for years. The stress was the cumulative impact of twenty years in the classroom, four years of invasive infertility treatments, and a major move from one neighborhood that had been home for nine years to a new home in a new town with a much longer commute. No doubt, my expanding collection of physical clutter was a major contributing factor to this "perfect storm" brew I had created as well. I was forty-two years old at the time, a mother, a wife, a teacher, and I was burned out! I didn't know who I was anymore or what I loved. I had lost my rudder and all contact with my heart's longing. I had lost my way.

Sometimes we're so caught up in our heads that we need a major shake-up to get our attention. My healing crisis that winter showed me that I was seriously out of step with my true self. I knew that if I didn't address these early warning signs—like, *pronto*—things could get a lot worse.

So I did the unimaginable and gave notice. I walked away from the relative comfort of a senior position, a monthly paycheck with full benefits, a community that had been family to me, and leapt head first into the terrifying void of not knowing. Yanking the plug was no small achievement for someone so tightly wired to a daily routine, a professional identity, and financial security. All I could do for the first few months after quitting was grieve for the old parts of myself that I was deliberately dismantling—unaware that my little sore throat was like a pebble that started an avalanche of clearing and transformation that continues to this day.

I know of no handbook that shows us how to deconstruct, and re-shape a life, no natural follow-the-dot sequence that takes us gently by the hand from point A to B. For a year after I left teaching, I simply followed my nose and improvised my life, sometimes making lame stabs at clearing out a drawer, sometimes doing things that made my heart sing, sometimes doing things that made no sense at all. There was no particular pattern or unifying principle or plan. I allowed my little dinghy, now repaired and in much better shape, to float along looking for the next strong current. That new current came in the form of an innocent query and the unexpected gift of a book.

These pivotal encounters that galvanize us have a way of sneaking in the back door. In the first of these two encounters I was asked if I had a business card. I'm thinking: *Business card? Me?*

But this innocuous request did something to me. It unleashed a host of unexpected and energizing possibilities. *Hmmm ... a business card.* The question challenged me to consider what my card would say if I had one to give out to people. It tapped into the place that knew all along: my heart. *Tending the Home ... Nourishing Homes ... Beautiful Home Spaces ... Healthy Spaces ... Healing the Home ... Feeling at Home ... Flowing Home ... Sanctuary ...* The phrases flickered on and off like little neon signs as my mind scanned the airwaves for answers to what my ideal life and new identity might look and feel like. It felt really good to play with new ideas, to wake up to possibility. All that aimless floating suddenly felt like directed floating.

It's a simple exercise. Give the brain one question to chew on and it can take you places you never imagined possible. Massaging sentence fragments to design my tagline had a delicious way of connecting the dots of my life that spanned forty-plus years of experience, beginning with my home-making marathons for my dolls and teddy bears when I was a child, and my experiential side-studies in metaphysics when I was a teenager. The business card question took me as far back as I could remember and revealed a whole new direction that I was quietly and unknowingly cultivating. Things began to make some sense.

Just days after this big moment of clarity, a book about clearing spaces was delivered un-beckoned to my front door by someone I barely knew. "Thought this might interest you," read the accompanying note. It still amazes me how I get what I need when I need it.

If the business card exercise was like receiving a special key, my being offered a book about space clearing felt like I was being shown the first doorway to which the key offered special entry. This one gateway would lead me down a path to the next threshold, and the next, revealing new openings only when I was ready to understand and live them. These pathways covered a lot of ground and were not always comfortable or easy. But they took me places that I could never have planned, orchestrated, or predicted if I had tried.

Bundled together, the highlights that span the last decade of my life could easily read like the catalog of study of a self-organized, non-linear, graduate program. I like to think of these extraordinary opportunities not so much as a summary of my professional re-invention, but as part of larger, on-going journey of self-discovery.

In the course of ten years I would complete an intensive one-year program in women's spirituality, study with the oldest living Reiki master, and develop a simple stress-relieving practice in yoga and meditation that my low tolerance for these things could sustain.

I would train for eight years with the world's leading experts in the field of personal and environmental space clearing, dowsing, and clutter clearing, and complete two uniquely different, multi-year certification programs. I would build a Web site and open a private practice dedicated to bringing homes and workplaces (and the people who occupy them) back into balance. I would live in Mexico for six months and peel away even more layers by exploring the shadow aspects of growing up there. I would teach again.

I would clear more clutter than I ever imagined possible. I would get to know and re-visit many of my old limiting beliefs that supported a lifetime habit of holding on. I would learn to accept Mystery as a legitimate state of being.

I would continue to grow every day by being a mom to my daughter, a partner to my husband, and a steward to my home.

And finally, the biggest surprise for me of all: I would discover writing as the perfect way to process my journey and tell my story; the perfect outlet for that teacher in me who gets a rush every time she finds the key that unlocks an "ah-ha" moment. I would write the book that might inspire others to go for it and take the "clearing plunge."

So here it is, unveiled at long last, from my home to yours: a book written by a teacher who is very much—and always will be—a student on the clearing path. A book that combines the ancient wisdom of space clearing with the modern practicality of clutter clearing—in a way that everyone can relate to, use, and enjoy *every day*.

May this book reveal rich insights every time you read (and re-read) it. May it help you soften and release some of the colorful ways you hold on. May it guide, inspire, and support you to discover who you truly are.

And, may gentle breezes prevail on your journey.

Introduction

Change happens slowly and then all at once.
—Unknown

Your Spacious Self

It seems we spend half our lives winding ourselves up, like mechanical wind-up toys, and the other half of our lives unwinding, or trying to unwind. If we've learned to live well, our unwinding will be even and steady. We'll have energy to spare right up to the very end. If we've wound up our "toy" too tightly or too fast over the years, however, we'll either find ourselves stuck in a lock jam that keeps us spinning in circles, or we'll unwind so fast that we'll career off the table, hit the wall, and keel over.

This book shows you how to unwind the slow and steady way.

But it also teaches this little mind-bender: *You are not the wind-up toy.*

Behind the coiled-up mess that is your stress and your clutter there is an infinitely spacious place one might call stillness, or joy. This is our natural state of being, but we hardly know it because most of us are caught in a tangle of worry, fear, negative beliefs, material attachments, and endless, mechanical "doing."

This book invites you to embark on an adventure of discovery as you gently unwind and shed the layers of your tangled self. You know which self I'm talking about: that grumpy, overwhelmed, and fragmented self that has lost the ability to live fully and think big; the self that is fully padded with all kinds of protections and stuff to ward off the calamities which are certain to come at any moment; the self that feels like there is more to this thing called life, but can't seem to figure out where it is and how to find it. Yes, these are the layers that will be melting away.

Believe it or not, behind all that padding is a very rich and spacious being, a new self that is juicy and whole, grounded and present. This self can be innocent and curious like a child, deeply happy like a dog on a walk in the woods, giddy like an explorer who has just found hidden treasure, or content and complete like a grandma sitting in her rocking chair recounting stories of her remarkable life. This self lives in awe and wonder. To this self, everything looks and feels new, and fresh, sparkly and amazing—and clear!

Actually, this self is not really all that new—it's just new to you! This new, bigger, self has been there all along, patiently waiting on the sidelines to come out and play. I'm sure you've experienced her or him in flashes from time to time. This self is the one that laughs a lot, doesn't take everything so seriously, and has a lot more fun.

So, welcome to the new you! You are about to uncover the divine mysteries of your most alive and spacious self!

If You're Human, This Book is for You

Don't let the word "clutter" in the title fool you into thinking that this book is written only for those of us who suffer from physical excess. If you're one of those tidy, organized, neat-as-a-pin types, this book is for you, too. In fact, no matter what your housekeeping habits and lifestyle predilections might happen to be, if you live in a body that gets out of balance, thinks thousands of thoughts a day, feels pain and loss and fear from time to time, or gets caught up in worries of the moment, this book is for you.

First of all, in this book the word "clutter" refers to anything that gets in the way of experiencing your most spacious self. This definition of clutter is much broader than usual, and includes the myriad ways we hold on and create imbalance in our lives. This book will help you identify your particular brands of holding on. I'm sure you have one or two issues kicking around somewhere; if not in your home, most likely they lurk somewhere in your life.

Second, there's being "clutter free" and there's being "spacious." These are not always synonymous. The difference is between thinking of yourself as a wind-up toy that needs to be unwound, and *knowing* that you are something way more, way bigger, than that. This book is intended to help you move beyond the veils, beyond the limiting beliefs of who you perceive yourself to be and what you think is possible.

Though I try my best not to make any promises, it's fair to say that you will experience your most spacious self if you're willing to feel the feelings that come up when you clear. Our body with its five primary senses is one of the most powerful resources we have for giving us feedback, should we choose to pay attention to it.

At the same time, I can predict that you might also experience your most contracted self, since clearing at any level has a sneaky habit of pushing our buttons. As we slowly dismantle the crusty armor of our holding patterns, the ego part of us that is attached to our comfort and everything else—including the kitchen sink—might squirm and blow a few gaskets. You'll recognize this when you feel yourself getting cranky, tired, spacey; you'll want to avoid, over-eat, or hold on even more. You'll recognize the ego-part when you hear your inner critic find every reason to discredit your efforts, convince you that this clearing thing doesn't work for beans, and that this book is probably the worst one you ever read. If any litany of judgments derails you, remember: *This is the "clutter part" of your mind talking, not the real you!* The first step is to try not to give in to all that noise.

Another one of the points with which the small self might take issue is the notion that the practice tools are just "way too easy." It is amazing how much our little toddler minds like to complicate our lives. When offered a way through that is extraordinarily simple, we balk. Hand us the keys to the kingdom, and we think there's got to be a catch. It can't possibly be this easy! Again, memo to self: *clutter talking.* Our cluttered minds have zero concept of simple.

This book is a journey of "shedding layers by shedding light" in ways that do not stir up a fear response. The slow-drip approach to clearing in this book may seem aggravatingly slow and maybe even trivial, but your level of success depends entirely on trusting and sticking with the program, *no matter what your wind-up toy has to say about it.*

Clutter Is a State of Mind; Clearing Is a Way of Being

"Spaciousness?!? You've got to be kidding. I can't even get past the piles of paper and the junk in my basement, let alone talk about spaciousness!" This is what many of my clients and students are saying, or at least thinking about, when I go into my song-and-dance spiel on the bigger picture. Do any of these thoughts ring true for you?

- No matter how hard I try, I just can't seem to manage the sheer volume of stuff.
- I've bought the books on clutter clearing; I've smudged my entire house with sage; I've practiced some of the suggestions on simplifying that I read in *Real Simple*; I'm hooked on TV's "Clean Sweep" … but my clutter just creeps on back, like a nasty weed.

- It's easy for me to get rid of stuff, it's my husband (wife, mom, child …) who has a hard time letting go of things, or, [variation] who *doesn't even see* the piles.
- I've spent gobs of money on closet systems, containers and baskets, professional organizers, even therapy … but my clutter remains a source of pain, shame, and embarrassment.
- My office desk is perfect. My desk at home is a disaster.
- I'm a neatnik. I control my chaos with order.
- What will become of me if I let this thing (thought, relationship, resistance, worry, status symbol) go?
- My stuff needs me.

You're not alone. Despite the proliferation and popularity of how-to books, magazines, make-over reality television shows, *Feng Shui* cures, closet organizing services worth billions of dollars a year,[3] and a self-storage industry that is bigger than McDonalds, Burger King, and Wendy's combined,[4] clutter continues to grow, quickly becoming one of the biggest epidemics of our time. There is no denying that our stress and our stuff is burying us alive!

Underlying the dizzying facts is the unrelenting message that if we simply banish this curse we will finally find true heaven on earth. The standard view sees clutter as a "thing" that is separate from us: a nuisance or growth that we must extract, conquer, outwit, or reorganize back into orderly piles. And, like a strict diet that that must be endured, clearing is considered about as compelling as a root canal.

So what gives? With all the attention given to the problem, why is it that our homes and lives are still so stressed, stuck, and out of balance? What's missing from this equation?

As we have touched upon already, clutter is not separate from us, and neither is it who we are. Yes, it shows up in our life as a physical nightmare of unsightly piles and disorganized messes (or in my case, as controlled chaos). But if you really think about it, clutter didn't begin that way. Clutter didn't just crawl into the house all by itself.

What most clutter clearing modalities do not recognize is that clutter—*before* it becomes something tangible that spills out of our closet or trips us in the basement—exists in another, more invisible form.

Clutter has to begin somewhere. That somewhere is a gestational unit with a built-in continuous "on" switch called the human mind. Our negative thoughts and our fear-based attitudes beget clutter, and that clutter spawns more clutter, thanks to the universal laws of attraction and resonance. How you construct your life, and with what and whom you choose to surround yourself, *out there*, has everything to do with what is going on—*in here*—in your mind. There is no separation.

Most traditional approaches do not consider the energetic impact of clearing, no matter how miniscule the task or effort. The fact is, clearing anything consciously and gently, as this book teaches, creates an energetic opening—a spaciousness—that works on us slowly and surely to soften our grip of attachments. You are more likely to throw in the towel just when things are beginning to shift, quietly, under the radar of any discernable progress. You might lose faith precisely when you should *not* be giving up and giving in to the agitations of the ego—the part of you that is only concerned with your comfort and keeping things the way they are.

What most people do not recognize is that the simple act of clearing one little thing with intention, every day, is more powerful and sustainable than binge-clearing a whole lot of things on the fly. By consistently clearing something small like a purse, a wallet, or even just one paper clip off your chronically messy desk, you can bypass your brain's fight-or-flight wiring system to such a degree as to create a sea change—a clearing movement of global proportions!

Another reason why many methods of clearing and organizing do not work is that they promote an active and linear process of clearing, like a problem to be fixed, managed, or solved. In our Western culture where "action" reigns supreme, if we can't "do something" or "make something happen," *now*, then we are wasting our precious time. Going slowly and waiting to see what happens is a hard sell for those looking for immediate results. These linear approaches completely dismiss, and miss, the equally powerful receptive elements of clearing that invite us to slow down, allow, listen, surrender, feel, soften, *let go*.

Most clearing efforts do not make room for us to feel our feelings, honor our ebbs and flows, create a container of safety, embrace our shadow side, or allow us to be more compassionate with ourselves. The *modus operandi* focuses on the end result, not the journey; on our intellect, not our innate wisdom; on throwing away, not letting go.

Until we begin to make a shift in our mindset that recognizes and embraces and includes the feminine aspects of clearing, we will not begin to change our lives, nor bring change to the planet. It is, in fact, this more balanced treatment that takes us beyond clutter-freedom into the vaster territory of our most spacious self.

Radical in its simplicity, this paradigm shift in clutter clearing is really good news for everyone, including those who believe they don't have any clutter at all! As the chart below illustrates, this book is an opportunity to consider a whole new way of thinking about your clutter and a new meaning for how to clear it.

CHART: A Paradigm Shift in Clutter Clearing

Clutter and Clearing: The Old View	Clutter and Clearing: A New View
1. Clutter is solid matter: physical and visible.	1. Clutter is stuck energy that manifests first as thought, word, and deed.
2. Clutter is separate from us.	2. Clutter is an extension of us.
3. Clutter grows like a weed.	3. Clutter grows as a result of human unconsciousness.
4. Clutter is bad, a nuisance, something to be ashamed of.	4. Clutter is a teacher; it reflects the places in us we have yet to love and heal.
5. Clearing is a linear process.	5. Clearing is a journey.
6. Clearing is pushing through resistance and "throwing away."	6. Clearing is softening resistance and "letting go."
7. Clearing is a mindless, tedious exercise.	7. Clearing is a mindfulness *practice.*
8. Clearing is about making a change.	8. Clearing is about *allowing* a change.
9. Clearing can be used to bury and deny our feelings.	9. Clearing can be used to allow and experience our feelings.
10. Clearing creates a pathway to our door.	10. Clearing creates a pathway to our most spacious self: the compassionate heart.

What to Expect

This book is divided into two parts, which offer the concepts, tools, and practice of clearing visible and invisible clutter. Collectively their purpose is to:

- Raise your awareness about what clutter is and how it blocks who you are;
- Soften your hardwiring around attachments to things, beliefs, and outcomes;
- Inspire, nourish, and support you as you grow into, and inhabit your most spacious self.

In Part I, "Different Faces of Clutter," we will explore how we get so out of balance in the first place by examining the nature of human perception and consciousness. We will take clutter down to the studs and view it from three different angles: as imbalance, as perception, and as energy. At the conclusion of each of the first three chapters you will be given an opportunity to "Tune In" to the clutter in your life and experience it directly using your six senses. Yes, by using this book, you will be developing your sixth sense of intuition and inner knowing as well as clearing your clutter.

In Chapters 4 to 9 in Part II, "The Journey of Clearing," you will have an opportunity to ease into new habits of clearing in six stages. Each chapter features specific "Try This" exercises and concludes with a series of weekly clearing tasks called "Clearing Practice" and a series of discussion questions called "Clearing Circle." The latter two tasks comprise the workbook portion of this book. It is designed to help you direct your clearing efforts more purposefully. The self-guided Practice and Circle programs can be adapted easily into weekly, bi-monthly, or monthly segments depending on your needs and level of commitment.

The six practice stages—Feeling, Refocusing, Tending, Easing, Witnessing, and Enjoying—are your pathways to spaciousness. They are most effective when considered in the context of a larger, ongoing journey rather than as a specific end-result.

Chapter 10 integrates the six clearing segments into one recommended daily program with the aim of promoting a clearing lifestyle that is effortless, sustaining, and, hopefully, fun! The "Clearing Planner" template, which you will find in the Appendix to photocopy as many times as you wish, will help you organize your practice: Clarify your intentions, keep track of your weekly progress, and hold yourself accountable. You will also be guided each week to write down any "feelings, shifts, synchronicities, dreams, or ah-has" in a journal to help you see for yourself how things might be changing for you.

The Clearing Circle guidelines, outlined in Chapter 10, will help you create and maintain your own clutter clearing support group should you wish to go that route. I have learned from teaching my six-week workshops that sharing our stories of triumph and challenge with other fellow seekers is a powerful way to clear layers of invisible stuff. When we feel safe and heard, we are more inclined to let go. It often happens that my students feel lighter after a Circle gathering even if they haven't lifted a finger to clear when they get home! It is pure magic that way.

You will notice that I repeat certain terms a lot throughout the book. Words or phrases like "weather," "strings," "droppings," "stop and feel," "not knowing," "tolerations," and so on, might first appear in italics not to draw emphasis to them, but to indicate a new usage: an on-going concept, theme, or quality of being that I am trying to convey.

Expect this book to be loaded with opportunities to clear. If you're just getting started, this might feel a bit overwhelming. But if you follow one of the two basic approaches described in the next section and allow the book to guide you, you will do just fine.

How to Use This Book

There are two basic ways to use this book: there is the "toe-dipping" approach to clearing and there is the "diving in" approach to clearing. Toe dipping can involve following the book as you would a guide in a museum: stopping at any of the Tune In and the Try This exercises to get a taste of clearing. You can also do what I do sometimes: Ask a question like, "What is one thing I could do right now?" or "What message do you have for me right now?" and then open the book at random and see what it tells you. I'm a big fan of working with the quick hits I receive from my universe.

If you're really serious about making a change in your life and would love to feel more spacious more of the time, however, I highly recommend you dive in by following the Clearing Practice program in Part II. The Practice will take you much deeper than the toe-dipping alternative and will increase your chances of developing a clearing habit that becomes a way of life instead of just another passing fad or curiosity.

If you feel you would benefit from sharing your clearing experiences with others and could use the support and encouragement, I recommend you organize a Clearing Circle in your hometown or neighborhood. The simple steps for how to begin and maintain your own group are fully detailed in Chapter 10. If you already belong to a book group or support group, consider taking a six-week or six-month "side trip." Or ask some of the members with whom you feel most comfortable if they'd be interested in joining you on a clearing journey. If you can't find anyone to join you from your immediate circle of friends, put an ad in your community newspaper or convene a clearing group by going online to sites like "Meetup.com"[5] and see if it generates any interest.

Whichever method you decide to adopt, the important thing to remember is to keep moving! If the detailed explanations of clutter in Part I are bogging you down, making you antsy to get on to the clearing experience, feel free to skip right on to Part II. Your success does not hinge on your understanding (or buying) the principles behind my clearing program. At the very least, however, I recommend you read all of Chapter 1, as it will introduce the key concept of *weather*, which is a powerful tool that I use to explain how we can detach from our holding patterns.

Similarly, do not let one clearing task throw you off track. If a task doesn't do it for you, move on to the next one. If you begin to feel overwhelmed and disheartened, notice this simply as an emotional weather pattern that has kicked up. The point is to move through it as best as you can. By the time you reach Chapter 10, you will have had an opportunity to experience and integrate the practice tools so completely that you may notice new habits of clearing naturally creep into your life when you least expect it!

Keep in mind that it is the nature of clutter—in all its creative manifestations—to find ways to derail our clearing efforts. Resistance comes built-in as part of the package. Expect it.

It takes a lot of courage to embark on an adventure into the mystery of your deepest self. My best advice is that you keep your sense of humor, keep it simple, and have fun! As you will learn in Chapter 2, there is no such thing as separation. Your clearing practice may feel unique and solitary to you, but your efforts, large and small, benefit us all on the planet in ways we cannot even begin to fathom! Your clearing is our clearing. Hang in there!

Part I

Different Faces of Clutter

♋

If you understand, things are just as they are.
If you do not understand, things are just as they are.
—Zen Koan

Chapter One

Clutter as Imbalance

It's terribly amusing how many different climates
of feeling one can go through in a day.
—Anne Morrow Lindberg

Going to the Goodwill

In the past ten years of clearing clutter, I have had bouts of feeling totally lost and longing for those comfortable parts of myself that I have released, even though I know in my heart they no longer serve me. My clearing anxiety has been so great at times that I have found myself on the verge of asking for some of my things back—from friends, from the Goodwill attendant, from the consignment clerk.

I have driven away from a consignment store completely bereft, analyzing to exhaustion the myriad of scenarios under which I could have made good use of the object or outfit I have just given away.

I know it was too small, but was it?

My inner state of mind is such you'd think I was Sophie in the movie *Sophie's Choice*, giving up one of her kids to the Nazis. This anxious diatribe lasts anywhere from fifteen minutes to twenty-four hours. After that, I find that the "fever" usually breaks and I get on with my life without as much as a backward glance.

Not all of us are like this (or this bad), of course. But I would wager that most of us have a very special brand of holding on.

What is your thing? What might your special "grip drama" look or feel like to you? Under what circumstances do you notice yourself holding on so tightly that, as Lama Surya Das describes it, you get "rope burn?"[6] In what ways do you block and resist the whole being that you are?

Here's how one of my holding patterns has played out more times than I care to admit. I call it the "death march to the Goodwill truck," a drop-off trailer which is permanently installed in the back corner of our supermarket parking lot. The scene is this: I stuff the trunk of my car with huge garbage bags full of clothes and shoes, handbags, kitchenware, old sheets and towels, and drive them two blocks to the trailer with a mix of eager determination, relief, and dread. I force myself to chant my mantra: *Ahh, this is going to be great ... I can do this ... no big deal ... it's easy ... see ...*

I feel tension beginning to build inside of me.

As I pull my car up to the truck I am rocked by the familiar jolt: *Ohmygod, I can't give away the beautiful green hoodie jacket my baby girl wore for three years. I can see her running and laughing in that thing with her curls bobbing out of the hood. It's in such perfect condition ... And those cute baby shoes! Maybe I could make some kind of art mobile out of them and hang them in my house somewhere. I've seen people hang them on their rear view mirrors or coat them in bronze ...*

Yet again, my monkey mind[7] has completely taken over....

... I could use those sheets for ... well ... don't know what ... oh yeah, the mummy costume we talked about. I know they'll come in handy one of these days (as they sit in the basement mildewing). *And the earrings I got from my grand-mother* (and never wore) ...

And so it goes ...
I don't think I can do this!

I force myself out of the car and make my way to the trunk, palms sweating. *Breathe, Stephanie, keep breathing ...*

I search for that jacket in the bag and pull it out. *I can't give this up ... She was so cute in it ...* (Holding up to my nose) *... Oh, and it still has her smell, her joy, her energy ... I can't give away that smell!* I tuck the jacket into the way back of the trunk where the attendant won't see me.

I hand the rest of the bags over to the attendant. I feel unsteady, nauseous. My wavering resolve is becoming a big heap of mush on the pavement. I grieve ... *I hate this, I can't stand this feeling! I feel so sad, so empty, so ...* uh ... wait a minute....

And then it happens.

It's an itty-bitty wee awareness that nudges itself through the ego-mind's fear-lock. Almost imperceptible ... *Yes, is it possible? Do I feel even a teensy bit lighter ...? Can it be that I'm able to breathe just a little easier?*

I take in my first deep breath since I come home. *It's OK. I survived. I made it.* It almost feels good.

Later I think, *What the heck was all that drama about!* My daughter's jacket goes right back into the give-away box for the next time I take a carload over to Goodwill. I think I finally did let that one go … after about five tries.

Clutter as Weather

Many Goodwill adventures later, I am slowly but surely learning to separate out the noisy dramatics and heart palpitations from the more peaceful, go-with-the-flow acceptance. I now see these dramas as holding patterns that are part of a larger "weather system" that is unique to me. I've become so aware of the passing nature of these patterns—like clouds moving in and out, or squalls intensifying and easing—that I now reframe any event, emotion, or physical sensation that does not reflect my most even-minded, spacious self: It's simply *weather.*

Sweaty palms, weather. Shallow breathing, weather. Worry that I made a mistake, weather. Worry that they don't make outfits like the one I just gave away, weather. Worry that someone will not care for my old laptop as well as I have, weather. Worry that I'll never find another one like it, weather. Memory of having something taken away from me as a child, weather. Grieving loss, weather. Tears, weather. Fear for the future, weather …

Contrast those patterns with: acceptance, *not* weather. Trust that there is more where that came from, not weather. Spacious non-attachment, not weather. Witnessing the weather, not weather. Pure, clear and uncluttered, these states of being are the real deal.

Your Weather Map

If you were to draw the weather patterns of your life, like the ones you see on TV, what would your weather map look like? Would your map stay fairly constant every day or would it change from moment to moment? Would it be mostly high pressure systems with occasional lows moving in? Or is your life mostly a series low pressure days bringing in unstable systems all the time?

Do you wake up to gray and cloudy skies in the morning and find that the fog has lifted after your first or second cup of coffee? Does your day begin as bright and sunny only to darken noticeably with your commute or another battle with your teenage son? Does the crazy driver who squeezes you out of your lane, causing you to spill your coffee, add lightning and thunder rage to an already threatening landscape?

As a witness to your own daily weather patterns, what do the bright, spacious skies in your life feel like? How about endless days of gray? How long before a big storm comes in to rattle your windows and flood your basement? Are your storms big and flashy, lasting only a few minutes, or are they on slow simmer throughout the day? Are your storms more of the wet (emotional) kind or dry kind? Are they loud and noisy? Are they quiet, then explosive? What color are they? What do they *feel* like?

If you think about it, the sun does not get pissed off because a few clouds muscle in to cover its fabulous view of the planet Earth. The moon is not attached to the changes in temperature that come when darkness sets in. Can you imagine a life where you become more like the moon or the sun—a witness to the storm rather than a participant in it? Where you don't take stuff personally? Where you become more at peace with whatever shows up on any given day?

Clutter clearing has a way of changing the weather patterns of our life, permanently. When we clear away our clutter, several things happen:

- We attract less "bad" weather.
- We are less affected by "bad" weather; it just becomes *the* weather as opposed to *my* weather.
- We begin to feel a sense of inner stillness and calm, like being in the eye of the storm, where life can batter the house, but the house itself stays strong and whole.

♍ Tune In: Feeling Weather Patterns

Below is a series of lists that lay out a wide spectrum of weather patterns. Presented in no particular order, these samples invite you to experience directly how clutter, like the weather, comes in many forms. Cover each list with a card or piece of paper and scroll down to reveal one line at a time. Notice how you feel after each item. At the end of the list take a moment to stop, close your eyes, and notice how you feel in general.

Notice if any of these patterns press your buttons, elicit sensation in the body, and/or trigger a memory, image, thought, or emotion. Once you've identified a feeling or a pattern, allow it. If you feel tears come up, for example, allow them. If you feel clammy, allow it. If you feel that your breathing is shallow, allow it. Don't try to analyze or fix anything. Just notice it. Feel it.

The first step in clearing clutter is to recognize the many ways clutter plays games with our energy level and mind. It is always important to remember that these weather patterns are not who we are and they actually do pass if we choose not to identify with them.

A word to the wise: Believe it or not, these lists have a powerful energetic signature. Words that are written down have as much power as if they were spoken. They can elicit strong physical and emotional reactions when we hold a charge around them. The purpose of this exercise is to become more aware of the places we hold on by simply observing (by feeling) any charge as a data point. If you find yourself feeling jangled, overwhelmed, distracted, tired, or even ill, stop the exercise and take a break. Drink a glass of water. Get some fresh air. Repeat to yourself, "It's not mine." If you don't feel a thing, that's fine, too. In the world of sensing, there is never a right or wrong answer, ever.

Physical Clutter

Physical clutter is the most familiar member of the clutter family because it is visible and identifiable; it's the stuff we see and wade through every day. Energetically, it is the grossest, densest form of holding on. Physical clutter is the end of the line. Because of its high visibility factor, the good news is that it can show us the way out!

Some faces of physical weather:

- ❑ Anything we don't use, love, or need
- ❑ Anything that we have yet to fix, finish, maintain, or fit (tolerations)
- ❑ Anything that does not have a "home"
- ❑ The piles, the mountains, the stacks, the towers, the boxes, the papers ...
- ❑ Dirt, grime, filth, mess, mold, mildew, cobwebs ...
- ❑ Stink, foul, putrid, dark, dusty, cloudy, scummy, dank ...
- ❑ Out of order, lost, broken, scratched, dismembered, mismatched, misplaced, disorganized, missing, stuffed, confused, scattered, spilled, stuck, chaotic, noisy ...
- ▪ *Stop and feel.* Close your eyes for a second. Notice any thoughts, feelings, and/or new weather showing up for you right now. Notice your breathing. Remember, there is nothing to do. Simply observe, allow, and experience these patterns as symptoms of imbalance.

Mental Clutter

Mental clutter is the incessant chatter generated by the small mind, or monkey mind. This is the domain of the resident ego barking orders to assure its eternal comfort and safety.

Some faces of mental weather:

- ❏ Negative thinking
- ❏ Negative self-talk
- ❏ Fear-based stories we tell ourselves
- ❏ Auto-pilot fears: "I should," "I can't," "I couldn't," "I shouldn't"
- ❏ Self-blame
- ❏ Motor-mouth endless chatter
- ❏ Over-thinking, over-analyzing, over-rationalizing
- ❏ Gossip
- ❏ Endless-loop tapes that we play that do not support us or lift our spirits
- ❏ Posturing, incessant blathering, yammering, harping …
- ▪ Stop and feel

Emotional Clutter

Emotional content by nature has an up and down quality to it. Unlike feelings, which are defined in this book as a way that we *respond* to information in our environment, emotions carry a greater energetic charge and are the way we *react* to our world of information.

Some faces of emotional weather:

- ❏ Nursing or holding a grudge
- ❏ Still mad at something that happened a while ago
- ❏ Guilty conscience
- ❏ Fear for someone or about something
- ❏ Reaction to an opinion
- ❏ "Poor me" victim mentality
- ❏ Hoarding
- ❏ Acting out
- ❏ Catastrophizing
- ❏ Strong attachment to an outcome
- ❏ Highs and lows
- ❏ Soap-box ranting
- ❏ Defensiveness
- ❏ Temper tantrum
- ❏ Moodiness …
- ▪ Stop and feel

Psychological Clutter

Psychological disorders are way bigger and more complex than I can do justice to here. For the purposes of highlighting patterns with which you might resonate, however, psychological clutter is presented as the result of unexpressed "shadow" material. When the shadow is not honored or embraced as a significant part of the whole being, it creates imbalance. The psyche is always doing whatever it can to restore balance, sometimes in explosive, disassociative, and dysfunctional ways. Dreams are a great way to explore this dark, uncensored, inner landscape.

Some faces of psychological weather:

- ❑ Denial
- ❑ Secrets, lying
- ❑ Feeling repressed, suppressed
- ❑ Hoarding
- ❑ Depression
- ❑ Biting critic, biting tongue
- ❑ Mind games
- ❑ Addiction: to food, alcohol, drugs, sex
- ❑ Bingeing, purging
- ❑ Stealing
- ❑ Panic attack
- ❑ Drug dependency …
- ▪ Stop and feel

Spiritual Clutter

The compassionate heart is the great unifier and healer, infinitely spacious, and not attached. This book defines spiritual clutter as anything that gets in the way of opening up to our source of innate wisdom and divine guidance.

Some faces of spiritual weather:

- ❑ Resisting deeper yearnings
- ❑ Resisting joy
- ❑ Feelings of loss
- ❑ Disconnection from Nature, wonder, and beauty
- ❑ Loneliness
- ❑ Rage
- ❑ Sense of entitlement
- ❑ Feeling small, powerless, insignificant, unworthy

❑   Separation mentality: "us vs. them"
❑   Polarized beliefs around religion, race, gender
❑   Worry that we're going to Hell
❑   Censorship
❑   Power over
❑   Terrorism
❑   Any-ism ...
▪   Stop and feel

Environ-Mental Clutter

The following are reflections of imbalances that show up in our environment and the planet at large.

Some faces of environ-mental weather:

❑   Disconnection from the earth
❑   Global unconsciousness, denial
❑   Global warming
❑   Global fear
❑   Pollution: skies, water, land
❑   Heavy metals, pesticides, toxic chemicals, synthetic hormones
❑   Geopathic stress: negative geo-magnetic fields, stress build-ups in the earth
❑   Irreversible climate changes
❑   Endangered species
❑   Production dehumanization: sweat shops, assembly-line unconsciousness
❑   Addiction to "more, "addiction to "faster"
❑   Judgments of all of the above ...
▪   Stop and feel

* * *

Summary: Clutter as Imbalance

- Clutter comes in many forms and has many faces.
- Clutter is any symptom of imbalance called "weather."
- Clutter has a way of showing you your buttons and pressing them.
- Any time your buttons get pressed by a person, place, or issue, it means that you are holding a charge.
- Observing (by feeling) the weather without attachment, releases charge.
- Clearing clutter has a way of changing the weather patterns of your life—permanently.

Chapter Two

Clutter as Perception

There is nothing either good nor bad, but thinking makes it so.
—Shakespeare, *Hamlet*

As Within, So Without

In the previous chapter, we explored the many ways that clutter expresses itself symptomatically, as weather. Now we will take our exploration a little deeper as we consider clutter from the point of view of perception: how what we see (or think we see) affects what we experience. Put another way, what we see, have, or experience at any given moment "out there" is directly influenced by what we generate "in here"—in our minds. In this chapter we will examine the extraordinary power of the mind to create reality. We will also see how it is linked to all other minds at the same time.

"But how does this relate to the junk in my garage?" you might ask.

In every way. The clutter in your garage had to begin somewhere. Chances are it grew out of some very old, unconscious beliefs or memories that continue to swirl unchecked in the ethers. In order to clear the stuff in our homes and lives we must consider and take responsibility for the thought forms, the perceptions, the emotional weather, that breeds all that physical stuff in the first place.

This chapter might feel a bit heady in places, but I invite you to stay with me. I touch on concepts that derive from Eastern spiritual traditions and quantum theory, not to give you a massive headache, but, hopefully, to give you a clear sense of how powerful you are. There is no tool or device required to create the joyous, spacious, clutter-free life you yearn for that doesn't already come built in to this amazing package we call the human body and this elastic generator we call the human mind!

There Is No Separation

One of the ways I like to explain the profound impact we have on one another and on the lives we create is to examine the concept of "no separation," which I introduce with a beautiful Hindu passage from the *Rig Veda*.

The *Rig Veda* is an ancient religious work of about two hundred and fifty hymns to Lord Indra, the king of the gods in Indian mythology. "Indra's Net"— the web of life that has at every juncture a jewel that reflects all other jewels—is a useful metaphor for the interconnection of all life in the universe, including universal structures like the Internet. This Eastern model predates particle physics by over 2,500 years! There appear to be several paraphrased versions of the hymn itself. This one by Frank Joseph is my favorite:

> "There is an endless net of threads throughout the universe ...
> The horizontal threads are in space. The vertical threads are
> in time. At every crossing of the threads there is an individ-
> ual. And every individual is a crystal bead. And every crystal
> bead reflects not only the light from every other crystal in the
> net, but also every other reflection throughout the entire uni-
> verse."[8]

The implications of an infinitely expandable, cosmic net that unites us all can be rather challenging to our limited self-concept. The mere idea that we are fundamentally not separate from each other—no "us and them," no "in here, out there"—can be mind-bending, to say the least. Imagine not being separate from our homes, our neighbors, the people in the next town over, or the next state, or the next continent. Imagine not being separate from the things that press our buttons, our worst enemies, or our clutter! Try, even just for a moment, to imagine these as a reflection and extension of our selves!

Investigative journalist, Lynne McTaggart, in her very readable book *The Field*, puts it this way:

> "There is no 'me' and 'not-me' duality to our bodies in relation to
> the universe, but one underlying energy field ... We are attached and
> engaged, indivisible from our world, and our only fundamental truth

is our relationship with it. 'The field,' as Einstein once succinctly put it, 'is the only reality.'"[9]

McTaggart takes the "new" scientific approach to describe the workings of this "pulsating energy field." She conveys this concept in a way that most non-scientific people like myself can actually understand:

> "In classical physics, the experimenter was considered a separate entity, a silent observer behind glass, attempting to understand a universe that carried on, whether he or she was observing it or not. In quantum physics, however, it was discovered ... that a participatory relationship existed between observer and observed—these particles could only be considered as 'probably' existing in space and time until they were 'perturbed', and the act of observing and measuring them forced them into a set state—an act akin to solidifying Jell-O. This astounding observation also had shattering implications about the nature of reality. It suggested that the consciousness of the observer brought the observed object into being. Nothing in the universe existed as an actual 'thing' independent of our perception of it. Every minute of every day we were creating our world."[10]

"Participatory relationship." There it is. These two words from McTaggart's passage hold gigantic implications. Two words that suggest that a *potential something* (atomic wave) becomes an *actual something* (atomic particle) when the thing they name is *observed!* Two words that imply a table, for example, doesn't materialize out of the ethers in isolation—just "because." It manifests only as it is imagined, observed, or intended. A chair, a car, a meal, a job, a parking space, a clear home ... These become form because we have given them our attention, our life force, our energy. They wouldn't exist without some degree of conscious or unconscious "participation."

It is breathtaking to think that all that we perceive out there is not only somehow intricately connected to us, but something that we have had a hand in creating in the first place. Quantum theory would suggest that the world as we see it—famine and feast, pestilence and prosperity, illness and health, war and peace, the Red Sox winning the World Series after eighty-six years—is implicitly shaped by our level of collective consciousness. Yes, even if these events are happening in some remote part of the planet far from where we are!

To illustrate this concept of "no separation" and "participatory relationship," I offer a simple story. It comes from my best teacher by far: my life.

Not long ago when I was on vacation I noticed that, not once, but in two very "separate" occasions, people around me suddenly started to howl in gales of laughter. You know, that kind of spontaneous side-splitting laughing where you double over and nearly pee in your pants? The kind of laughing that comes from being with best friends with no agenda, feeling pure ease, channeling pure joy.

The first time the laughter wafted over towards me at a restaurant I thought it was pretty cute. Two women sitting at the table next to us were laughing so hard they were crying. Between guffaws they would stop for a second to comment on how they must be disturbing the peace, only to dissolve again. I loved it and I wouldn't have thought any more of it, except for the fact that several hours later while I was walking with my husband by the beach, it happened again—with different people. The second time it was a happy threesome one-upping each other with a funnier quip that had the group rollicking in hysterics and collapsing on the boardwalk. It was contagious. It made me laugh, too, and it felt really good.

I've done enough observing in my life to believe that these two events were not just random quirks of nature. I couldn't help but think that somehow it was *my* frame of mind and state of being that had attracted this joyful energy into my day. Twice. It made sense. I was spending the day at a beachside resort. I felt very relaxed. I was in no rush to get anywhere. The food we ate was cooked to perfection. The ocean sounds, the smells, the breezes, were intoxicating. I felt calm and clear and happy. All was well in my world that day. I would even go as far as to say that I had created this level of spaciousness simply by being who I was at that moment in time.

You don't have to take my word for it. Try it for yourself. Think of a time you have felt most happy and at ease (without being medicated or under the influence of any substance). What was going on in your life around that time? Where were you? Who was there? What was going on in your mind? What were you feeling? Which of your five senses was most activated? Were you making it happen or allowing it to happen? Did you stage the experience and have a plan? Or did it just unfold on its own?

This is what I tell my students and clients: If you ever wonder how you're doing in your life, all you have to do is open your eyes and take a good look. Examine the cosmic net around you: your home, your job, your community, the people sitting at tables near you in a restaurant. Notice the jewels in your life: your family, friends, neighbors, co-workers, strangers on the street, your thoughts, your reactions, your physical sensations. Notice if people are smiling more than frowning. Notice if they smile more if you smile more. Allow the world out there to act as your mirror. Allow all those jewels surrounding you to reflect YOU back to you.

So, what is showing up on your movie screen of life?

You may be pleasantly surprised by what you see, and you may be surprised by what you have not wanted to see. If you aren't too impressed with yourself, imagine that it is possible to change the picture on your screen.

If we can wrap our limited little monkey minds around the notion that we ultimately create our reality "out there" by guiding our attention "in here," we can change just about anything. According to this paradigm, we can create more joy by allowing more joy, by witnessing more joy, by embodying more joy. We can have peace by *be*-ing peaceful! Now, this is a reality show to get excited about!

Polarizing Filters

If we're not separate in the bigger scheme, why is it that we can feel so distinctly separate? It's true, we're not the same people: We come from different corners of the planet, our dwellings are different, our languages, our behaviors, our preferences, our worldview. Even conjoined twins are different.

Not counting the obvious flesh-and-bone and geographical distinctions that make us the unique beings that we are, what keeps us feeling separate in my view, are the lenses and filters of our personalities. Our pretty little jewels are clouded over and obscured by the limited beliefs we have inherited, adopted, and experienced in our lifetime—no matter where we come from.

The mechanics of a simple camera is my favorite, non-scientific way of explaining how human perceptions shape our worldview. You don't need to know much about photography to know that the viewfinder of a camera will capture what it sees, and the shutter will click on a moment, freezing it in linear space and time. The more sophisticated photographer can manipulate and control the outcome of her images by increasing or decreasing the shutter speed, by adjusting the aperture, by adding different lenses and filters to her camera. By mounting a polarizing filter, for instance, she can remove some of the harsh glare to create a richer, darker, more textured shot. A telephoto or a macro lens can capture sharp detail, a fisheye lens creates an interesting distorted fishbowl impression.

Perception, by definition, implies "filter." What separates me from every other human being are the filters and lenses, the shutter speeds and apertures of my particular life package. My ancestral lineage, my DNA, my environment, my upbringing, my beliefs and memories, my fears and judgments, my parents' fears and judgments—all create the complex lenses from which I view my life experience. My stories, my preferences, my ideas about life, my ideas about this book have all passed through my own unique viewfinder and sieve, which I call "me." The fact is that my perception of me comes with all kinds of built-in filters and attachments that cloud and color my world from one moment to the next. How can it not? It's the human condition.

The thing is, as we grow (away from our true selves) we unconsciously *add* more filters based on the continued view that we are separate. Our "truth" begins to take on a life of its own the more we believe we are unworthy, the more we allow ourselves to be driven by what the collective decides is best for us, and the more we act out of fear and judgment. To the extent that any filters gum us up and *prevent* us from knowing and experiencing who we truly are, they become what the Buddhists would call obscurations. As you've probably gathered by now, I rather fancy the term from the previous chapter: weather, and the simpler, universal term, clutter.

Some filters come built in. For example, I can't get around the fact that I was born female and white. I am also heterosexual, a mother, tall, and I was born in Mexico in the 1950's. For better or for worse, what I experience will always come through these particular life lenses.

Then there are those filters that continue to be necessary to simply survive our life package. These are the defense-mechanism filters that have helped us feel safe in light of the harsher rays of painful memories, abusive life circumstances, or environmental stress. If I hear someone screaming at another person, for example, I'll spike a "fear-for-my-safety filter" and want to crawl into a hole as fast as possible. My reaction is so instinctive and immediate, like a squirrel scurrying to avoid a Mack truck. Because these intense flare-ups can feel so old and deep, my husband and I affectionately call them "dark surges."

The good news is that I am now able to identify the horror (weather) I feel when someone screams. It's still excruciating, and I still squirm, but I've gotten to the point where I can at least hang and *be* with it as a painful memory—a surge from a dark place within myself. As I allow myself to feel this weather without trying to analyze it, it begins to lose its charge and grip on me, little by little.

When you clear, it's not only wise, but prudent, to remove these lenses slowly and gently to the extent that your nervous system can handle the lighter rays of information. It may take a lifetime, but if you can at least feel the feelings without identifying with them, as this book teaches, you have come a very long way.

What do your inner lenses and filters look like? To what extent have you amplified, enhanced, distorted, blurred, cropped, or *polarized* the reality of who you are? What does your world look like through your rose-cluttered glasses? Better yet, what does it look like when they're clear?

Fear Factor

The human mind. It's the best drama machine around. It's portable. It runs day and night, even and especially when we're not aware of it or paying attention. It is infinitely expandable and requires only imagination to operate. It cranks out some of the best stories around. Just feed it a few tidbits of hearsay, half-truths, some emotional charge, some childhood memories (the more traumatic the better), and *voilá*, you're cooking, baby—with fire!

What we generate and experience depends entirely on what we feed our minds. Give the mind a story about terrorism in the country we're about to visit on vacation, and we've just generated a beautiful garden of fearsome delights complete with image of being robbed at gunpoint as we're stepping out of an ATM machine. Feed it more stories of earthquakes, poverty, and a recent airline crash, and we're probably dialing the number of our travel agent to cancel the trip, muttering incessantly under our breath: I ain't going nowhere!

A little freebie from the universe came to me as I was writing this chapter on perception. I was sitting at my desk ready to dive into my manuscript when I got a call from my daughter's middle school. "Your daughter was marked absent in homeroom today, is she sick?"

I'm thinking: *I just put the kid on the bus.*

In the never-ending five minutes that I waited for the administrator to call me back, I went from complete equanimity, *just a simple error,* to imagining the absolute worst, most horrific scenario of my daughter in the back seat of a car with a child molester.

My baby still in braces, fighting off the "perv" with her red monogrammed backpack!!

I felt the sickening feeling that parents feel when they learn that their child is missing. I felt the collective horror at the thought of inexplicable violations on a child. I felt my feeling so totally and completely to the point where I was hyperventilating, on the verge of throwing up. I could not imagine living after this.

How did I go from zero to one hundred miles an hour in no time flat? The mind can do some amazing things with very little data and evidence. In five minutes I had gone on a whirlwind tour of my worst nightmare, based on nothing more than an innocent inquiry and mistake.

But the most amazing thing happened. In the midst of my category-five hurricane, I was aware of a part of me that stood by, witnessing the whole thing with equanimity and no attachment. I watched how I went from complete calm to a madwoman ready to jump in my car and look for my daughter myself. I experienced the dark toxicity of this fear that surged through my entire body like a nuclear bomb had just exploded in my gut—a cancer in fast motion. I was aware of the intensity of these feelings and noticed that if I allowed them to continue to cycle, unmitigated, through my entire body, it could do some serious damage over time. I noted that my nervous system would not be able to sustain this level of abuse over the long term.

The school administrator did call back to reassure me there had been a mistake. My daughter had been in another classroom making up a missed test. It took me more than an hour to just calm down after the call. I still felt sick even though I knew things were OK. I wanted to blame someone for how awful I felt, but I knew there was no one to blame, not even myself.

In the end I realized that I had been given a huge gift. I was allowed to experience and feel my worst nightmare without actually having to live it in real life. I was given a chance to see how easy it is to lay the fear filters on really thick, and to notice what the body had to do to process the kind of information it was getting. I was given an opportunity to feel such compassion for those who have had to go through nightmares of this kind in their own lives.

What I gained from this jolting experience—yet another of the endless teachable moments—was a huge awareness of the awesome power we have as humans every moment of every day. If so little can create so much in the playground of the mind, what if we exercised some self-restraint and changed its daily diet! What if we consciously reframed a negative attitude or belief just once a day? What if we allowed our feelings—of pain, grief, or fear—to be just feelings, without acting on them or feeding them with more of the same? What if we could just witness an eruption without taking it seriously, or personally? If more of us practiced not identifying with just one little drama once a day, how might that change us, and, dare I say, our world?

The Neural Link

So what exactly was that explosion I felt in my gut? Why did it feel so visceral? How could it be so incapacitating? Why did it affect me for so very long after the event had already passed?

Inspired by the work of Dr. Candace Pert, author of *Molecules of Emotion*, here's how I might explain what's going on, as best as I understand it. If we were to take a human body while it processes the bio-chemical surges of a panic attack and look at it dispassionately through a microscope, the chain reaction might look something like this:

The external trigger is a phone call that delivers a message—perceived by this body as a threat. A growing wave of fear triggers a series of electrical impulses in the brain, which in turn sends out signals to different centers in the body to produce amino acids associated with a particular emotion—in this case, dread and panic. Once fired, the stress chemicals flood the body, seeking out their corresponding receptor sites—which I imagine as little wide-mouth Pac Man figures designed to feast on these chemical goodies.

The cells of the body, sensing the avalanche of amino acids, continue to "receive" them as long as they are being produced. And because of this bumper crop of Pac Mans specializing in dread and panic, this human has increased her chances of attracting a similar chain reaction the next time the school calls, or the evening news features a story about a missing child, or a black pick-up truck with darkened windows passes by on the street.

A pre-existing groove of reactivity has just grown even deeper.

The cascading reaction is how our bodies become hard-wired and addicted to all kinds of emotional weather patterns. Because of our constant identification with certain thoughts and beliefs, our bodies develop certain chemical predilections. The brain, unable to find an appropriate response to a given external stimuli, instead goes into an involuntary reaction every time there is a trigger.

There is a saying that states that neurons that fire together wire together. Even the slightest fear thought or memory, sound, or taste, can trigger the chain of events, which sets up the neural link. And once those chemicals are fired in the system it's already too late. Until we break the cycle through self-awareness, self-restraint, and feeling without personalizing, we will forever fall victim to our emotions. This is where reminding ourselves to repeat, "It's not mine" or "Don't go there"—a little bit every day—is a good start which can pay huge dividends over time.

Our Choice

Probably very few of us humans can look at an image of a battle, a politician, a chocolate bar, a starving child, a hurricane, or a gorgeous movie star, and *not* have an opinion about it—or a reaction. Our conditioning and body chemistry has us programmed to judge the image as being good or bad, positive or negative, right or wrong, better or worse. In fact, if we really paid attention, most of our thoughts are polarized or polarizing in one way or another. The famine in Ethiopia: bad; ninth-grade science teacher: bad (if he didn't have the comb-over he might be tolerable); the rain: good for the gardener/bad for the wedding, etc. Whatever the assessment, it simply becomes another filter and lens through which we view and create our reality.

Having a thought is just that—a thought. When we think it a lot, it becomes an opinion, which can grow into a belief. If it holds a strong charge, it becomes a judgment with its corresponding mix of potent chemicals in the body. In the end, our opinions and judgments aren't really who we are. They are simply *indicators of how far we have grown away from our true selves*, which, in case you've forgotten, is that we are not separate. Our highly charged thoughts and beliefs become the personality, the biology, and the lenses through which we experience our reality, and with which we've grown to identify for so long that we believe them to be real.

Even so, to the degree that we are not completely lost in our dramas, we can choose. We can choose to keep our heads stuck in the sand trap of illusion, adding more filters and stress chemicals to defend our position and prove our point, or, we can unplug. We can pull our perfect little pearl selves out of the shell, scrub them down, and see what's really shining beneath the static and noise. The clearing journey, should you wish to embark on it fully and consciously, will offer you the latter option, with full benefits.

♍ *Tune In: Feeling Charge*

Here's an opportunity to tune in to some of the "static and noise" (aka charge) you might be carrying. Without peeking, take an index card and cover the list of twelve words below. Uncover one word at a time and read or say it out loud, noticing what happens. Notice if any of these words press your buttons. Notice if they make you feel rattled, jangled, angry, stirred. Notice if you feel a surge of heat, greater thirst, increased heart rate, a momentary pang. Do nothing else but allow yourself to *stop and feel* any weather that is stirred by these particular lenses and filters. Remember, whatever you gather here is just another data point.

❑ Child with AIDS	❑ Fat	❑ Cancer
❑ Republican	❑ Nazi	❑ Hummer
❑ Pesticide	❑ Donut	❑ Binge drinking
❑ Shame	❑ Democrat	❑ Filth

♏ *Tune In: Identifying Belief Patterns*

When you can recognize that physical clutter as you know it began first as a belief pattern that has steadily grown unchecked over a lifetime, you can begin to dismantle it the same way it came: by feeling the charge that arises without personalizing it, and by reframing the thoughts that created it.

Below is a list of some of the top reasons we hold on. They are some of the more familiar lenses and filters we have inherited or adopted over the years. Notice if any of these resonate for you, press your buttons, or even spark a little humor. If you feel some weather coming through, of course, just observe and let it pass:

Scarcity Thinking 1: "Just in case"

This is probably the number one reason we hold on. It comes from a deep-seated belief that there is not enough to go around, the future is not to be trusted, and that life is just plain hard. Sometimes these scarcity patterns arise from bigger ones held and passed from generation to generation triggered by major events like "The Great Depression." The survival patterns of our pioneering forebears continue to be very much alive in many of us still, as seen by our little squirrel tendencies to hold on and store things just in case a swarm of locusts makes it impossible for us to venture outdoors. Holding on to those little bits of string and a basement full of Mason jars may have been necessary for the likes of Laura Ingalls Wilder to survive the harsh living conditions of her day in that little house on the prairie of hers. But unless caning and canning are your thing, hanging on for the eventual catastrophe that we fear will come at any moment only perpetuates an endless-loop cycle of more need and more lack.

Scarcity Thinking 2: "I told you so"

Yes, this is actually a reason we hold on. If it isn't enough to just hold and recreate a scarcity pattern, we also get to torment ourselves (or others) when the external reality proves our point. We get to beat ourselves up with over-rationalizations like, "See, I told you! I just knew we shouldn't have gotten rid of that computer, second bicycle, exercise machine (read: clothing rack), refrigerator, golf clubs …!" Some of us get real payoffs by perpetuating this victim consciousness and passive-aggressive behavior.

Shelf Life: "It's not used up yet"

This holding pattern comes from the belief that all matter of things, people, and experiences have a shelf life AND must continue to sit on the shelf for several decades until it is used up. "I want to get my money's worth" or "I spent a fortune on this" are also top reasons we hold on. The truth is that things can long outlast the real need for them. One way out is to imagine others enjoying the thing and passing it forward until its natural lifecycle is complete. Though the ego might cringe when I say this, we don't really "own" anything anyway. As Stuart Wilde, Taoist teacher and writer, simply puts it: "It's on loan to us from the God Force."

Sentimental Attachments: "This reminds me of ..."

This is a tough one for those of us who hang onto those sweet reminders of our past. It's things like your grandmother's candlesticks that you don't really love and never display because they have these hideous Gothic spikes; the roller blades you used as a teenager but cannot use anymore because they don't fit *and* you don't skate (!); the mildewed quilt that is beyond repair and reminds you of summers on Lake Champlain. By themselves these things seem so benign, don't they? The problem comes when they are part of a massive collection of sentimentalia, draining the life force right out of our home and lives. Choose a few based on love and honest usefulness and let the rest go.

Guilt 1: "Aunt Dorothy (God rest her soul) would kill me"

This is a biggie for those of us who believe that we are honor-bound to carry forth the traditions left by our beloved ancestors. The seventeenth century wingback chair *must* be carefully and prominently displayed because Grandpa did it, and his grandpa before him. Forget about the fact that it's painful to sit in and will crack under the weight of anyone over forty pounds. We live in terror that our dearly departed will actually pop out of his grave and grab us by the throat if he finds out that we sold his beloved treasures on eBay. Take a few photos to put in the album for future generations. Write a loving summary describing the item and what it meant to you. Of course, naturally, if *you* adore the thing, keep it. Repair it, display it, and enjoy it for *your* sake, not Aunt Dorothy's!

Guilt 2: *"This stuff needs me"*

Some of us think of our things as members of the family. Giving away the old laptop is akin to giving up a child for adoption to some unknown, less capable, foster parent who cannot possibly care for it as well as we have! "I can't possibly throw this away until I find the right home for it" is an excellent delay tactic, and for those of us with major control issues, rests high in the pantheon of holding patterns.

Emptiness: *"If I get too clear, there will be nothing left of me"*

Many of us live in fear that if we give up our things, a deep, black hole of emptiness will set in. What will become of me if I let this go? For some of us, giving up our stuff is so incapacitating that you'd think we'd been stranded alone, chained, and naked on a deserted island. The feelings of Loss run really deep. If I've learned anything about this particular holding pattern, it is not a fear of lack (as we saw earlier in "Scarcity Thinking"), but the weather of grief moving in that is so paralyzing. Here's the good news for those of us who feel these swells so acutely: clearing our things—slowly, gently—offers us the perfect opportunity to feel and heal the experience of Loss. Honor and acknowledge the objects (behaviors, relationships) you are releasing. Thank them, bless them, acknowledge what they meant to you. Creating a special ritual or altar of letting go can help soften the hardwiring (see Chapter 5). Reward each clearing effort by doing something that makes your heart sing.

Control: *"I am the master of my domain, in charge of all I survey."*

This belief is born out of and combines the previous two patterns: "This stuff needs me" and "If I get too clear, there will be nothing left of me." Clutter gives us the illusion of power. It is also a great way to passively piss people off. The piles of newspapers collected from the 1980's make us feel invincible. Junk strewn everywhere, helter-skelter, gives us something to control, manage, survey. It gives us a reason for being. If it weren't for all the stuff we pile up around us that makes us feel safe—like thick castle walls *and* moat—we might become vulnerable and even spontaneously combust! Getting rid of anything, including the useless pencil nubs, will wreck havoc on this delicate balance we have created. This control pattern, which results from a build-up of unexpressed rage, is like a house of cards. The underlying belief teeters dangerously on the edge of self-destruction if the tight coils that support it are not softened with high doses of self-acceptance and self-care.

Denial: "I don't want to have to feel those feelings"

"Denial" is the yang (more active) version of the "Emptiness" pattern described earlier. Denial protects us from having to do the unthinkable and feel those feelings. When we're too afraid to be alone with our feelings, we might choose a special brand of protective covering. Besides becoming clutter control-freaks we might become motor-mouth talkaholics. We might eat ourselves to near comatose just to avoid the nagging feeling of grief or loss. Pain medication, alcohol, drugs, sex, hoarding, these avoidance strategies that give us a false sense of security are deeper and more destructive form of weather. Memo to self: Start slow, allow your feelings, and exercise extreme self-care.

Sense of Belonging: "Makes me feel like I fit in"

We often hang onto stuff because it gives us an inflated feeling of importance. Those fancy designer shoes that no longer fit us at least make us feel as though we rate. If I hold onto that stinky torn-up t-shirt from the 1972 Rolling Stones concert (that I never wear), I get to prove to the world that I was there. And then there's the boyfriend I can't give up because he's cool, forget about the fact that he mistreats and disrespects me. If you must, take a photo of it (him, them) and let it (him, them) go! Then use the photo in a ritual of letting go.

Collective (Un)consciousness: "If 'everyone' is doing or having it, then it must be OK."

It's easy to go into denial when the collective culture supports a way of life that can be harmful or damaging to our bodies, homes, environments, and lives. If *everyone* eats fast food, then it must be OK. If everyone uses pesticides to make their lawns a perfect weed-free green, then it must be OK. If everyone has a gas-guzzling SUV, then it must be OK. If everyone gets/does/has … Watch your own inclinations to do or have something that doesn't feel right to you. Just because someone else does it, or has it, doesn't mean that it is healthful and supportive *for you*. Pay attention and honor your feelings. Also watch your inclinations to judge those who do it or have those things. Your judgments of them are just as harmful!

Your Special Brand of Holding

Come on now, you must have one. Which version of these can you most relate to? What do your holding—or weather—patterns look like?

* * *

Summary: Clutter as Perception

- There is no separation: you are connected to every one and every thing.
- What you see "out there" is a reflection of what's going on "in here"— in your mind.
- Lenses and filters are the limiting beliefs you have inherited, adopted, and acquired in your lifetime; they cloud who you are.
- The human mind is a powerful generator that cannot be shut off; it can only be directed.
- Fear creates stress chemicals that flood the body and affect its chemistry.
- Judgments are an example of charge.
- The stronger the charge, the bigger the lens and the more polarizing the filter.
- Clearing slowly allows you to remove the protective filters in a way that your nervous system can handle.
- To have joy and peace out in the world you must first embody joy and peace within.

Chapter Three
Clutter as Energy

When all is said and done,
we are nothing but vibration in a sea of living, intelligent energy.
—Belleruth Naparstek, *Your Sixth Sense*

Every Thought and Every Thing is Vibration

As we have seen, clutter manifests in a myriad of ways. It is visible and invisible. It is symptomatic of imbalances called weather patterns. It is the complex system of filters and lenses that make us feel separate and cloud our perceptions. In this chapter, we will be looking at clutter at its most elemental, as *energy*, to better understand how it shows up physically in our lives.

Though clutter appears to us as solid matter, if we reduced it to its smallest discernible parts, it is nothing more than atomic particles with a frequency and intensity, or, as the famous yoga master Paramhansa Yogananda describes it in his teachings: "congealed light." Japanese scientist, Dr. Masaru Emoto, in his book *The Hidden Messages in Water*, puts it this way:

"You might think, 'Existence is vibration? Even this table? This chair? My body? It is indeed difficult to believe that things that you can pick up with your hands and examine—things like wood, rocks, and concrete—are all vibrating."[11]

Energy is not static or permanent. As waves, it keeps moving and changing, ebbing and flowing. It forms and un-forms and *informs*. Matter is constantly changing back into energy and energy into matter. Energy holds no grudges. It doesn't care if you're having a bad day. It is neither good nor bad. It just is— pure potential, pure expression, pure attraction. As we learned in the previous chapter, where the mind goes, energy flows. When we invest pure potentiality with our thoughts and feelings, it becomes form. When we are aware of it as information, it gives us feedback.

If we were to measure the energetic frequency of a junked car or road rage, we would probably find that these vibrate at a much different rate than objects or experiences that make us laugh or feed our soul. In energetic terms, objects that we don't use or love vibrate at a much lower frequency (fewer cycles per second) than things that make our heart sing. Fear and worry are lower and less coherent than peace or joy. Judgments are lower than observations. Patterns of holding on would be lower than the patterns of letting go. You get the idea.

Basically it all boils down to this: The more we hold on to a person, thing, or belief that no longer serves and supports us, the lower and denser the energy wave patterns that we vibrate and emit. When we surround ourselves with people and things that make our hearts sing, we effectively lighten up the heavier frequencies in our life, which in turn, create and attract greater coherence— what I call spaciousness.

Clutter Goes with Us Everywhere

Hanging out in a sea of low-vibrational information is akin to having invisible ball and chain, or strings, keeping us tethered and stuck.

So imagine this: One object that we don't use or love equals one invisible *string* that attaches itself to us. A painful memory that we have not healed or embraced equals another string. A negative thought equals another. Same negative thoughts and painful memories repeated over and over again equals many strings. Hoarding, addictions, unmitigated fear … energetic spaghetti! God help us if there were a special device that could illuminate the coiled-up mess of all of our attachments and a build-up of highly-charged stress patterns over the course of a lifetime. The cumulative effect of all these strings tangled together would be what I affectionately refer to as "Pigpen's cloud," after the adorable *Peanuts* character who walks around with his permanent cloud of dust.

Like with Pigpen, this clutter cloud goes with us everywhere we go until we clear it. This would mean that the clutter in the closet is going with us to the store, to work, to school, to bed, even if it is physically stored or hidden in the closet. Even if it is stored in one of those PODS containers or storage centers in the next county. Yes, even if it's hidden in your parent's attic one continent away!

All of our clutter goes with us everywhere. We sleep, we eat, we play, we live, we make love, we work with … our clutter! It becomes like another member of the family that we are feeding, housing, and lugging around with us. It costs us tremendous vital energy. It may not always be visible to us, but until it is cleared, it will always be there and affect everything we think about, everything we do, and everyone we meet. It's no wonder that we can feel so stuck and unable to move forward in our lives.

Strings and Droppings

The thing about our Pigpen cloud is that it doesn't just travel with us everywhere we go like a permanent backpack of information. This cloud of clutter has two other distinguishing features as well:

- It has a powerful magnetic field that attracts more strings like it to itself;
- It leaves behind an energetic trail of *droppings* for other beings to stick to.

Based on the Law of Attraction, which simply states that "like attracts like," what this means is that we attract at the level that we vibrate, all the time, twenty-four/seven.

Here's how it works: As we unconsciously move through time and space we call life with our cloud of strings, most of us will also leave an invisible energetic trail behind us much like a snail leaves behind its thread or residue. If our cloud is vibrating at the level of "worry," or "fear for the future" for instance, we will not only attract people, places and things that carry the exact same frequencies in their energy fields, but we will likely leave a signature trail of worry and fear as we go. We become more like walking-talking Velcro clouds sticking to each other and leaving a messy trail along the way. Charming, isn't it?

To put this in perspective, the opposite is also true. If we are vibrating at the level of love and gratitude, generosity, forgiveness, spaciousness, non-attachment, balance, and joy, we will leave a higher vibrational trail behind which some might experience as clarity. If we are so spacious and not at all attached, having reached the first stages of enlightenment, we will likely leave no trail at all!

Imagine the kinds of people, places and life experiences that we might attract if we consciously vibrated at higher levels. The key to remember of course, is that (to the extent we are aware) *we get to choose at every moment how we wish to show up, move through life, and what kind of trail to leave behind!*

Strings Attached

How many times have you gone into a big warehouse store feeling just fine and come out totally depleted? Or, maybe you're standing in the checkout line of your supermarket and suddenly feel a wave of emotion, like depression, worry about money, anxiety—something you weren't feeling before? Perhaps you walk into a room and feel disturbed for no particular reason. The fact is, most of the stress we feel in our lives *isn't even ours!*

Next time you suddenly feel a wave or pang of something that you weren't feeling just moments before, think again, and breathe it out with the words, "It's not mine." Stress patterns that are not ours become ours the instant we *identify* with them. More strings are added to our invisible cloud, and we have a big mess to sort out later—if we're lucky.

To see the effects that our clouds, strings, and droppings can have on a collective level, consider this scenario: Let's say you have a huge argument with your spouse and have not, or cannot, seem to resolve the tension between you by feeling and releasing the emotional charge you two are holding. Energetic charge or polarity is like the plus and minus of a battery. The intensity of the argument and the length of time it has been festering work together to determine the degree of polarity that the charge holds.

If there was a lot of intensity to begin with, your fight will have left a nice-size dropping in the space where you two had your argument. And if you are still vibrating unhappiness and tension, there will likely be some strings connecting you to this spot and to each other. Unbeknownst to either of you, along comes a woman you don't even know who's also having a bad day. Because this third person's bad day is vibrating at the same frequency as your earlier fight, she will very likely resonate with this particular field of disturbed energy (because of some unfinished business of her own—*read:* unloved parts of herself), have a mini-tantrum, and leave another nice-size dropping *right on top of yours!* You don't even know the woman, and she has just added more strings to your ever-expanding cloud.

So here's the thing: Unless the original energetic dropping is released (embraced, loved, felt), it will continue to attract more unconscious strings and droppings. The world, no doubt, is full of these highly-charged overlays of polarized activity and information.

To give you an idea of what these collective stress patterns might look and feel like, imagine a heavily populated city during rush hour. Throw in road rage, hundred-degree temperatures and lots of Pigpen clouds of perceptions and personal agendas. The area can begin to look like one of those world maps you see in airline magazines that show all those red swooping lines connecting different cities all around the world. And we wonder why we're so stressed, confused, and depressed, needing ever-greater amounts of alcohol, medications, and escape tactics to calm down our short-circuiting nervous systems! Imagine the effect we can have on any space when we clean up after ourselves by paying attention, softening our position, and neutralizing the charge we hold.

I had a houseguest once who gave me an unforgettable taste of what it's like to take everything with you after a visit. My friend, who practices living consciously, had not only packed up her suitcase, but had gathered all her strings and taken them with her when she left. The second she drove away, my house felt energetically completely clear, as if she had never been there! What remained were the good memories of a fun visit and her sheets to be washed. It was an astonishing effect, and one that you might not notice at all if it weren't for how most spaces feel—cluttered, heavy, stuck.

Because we are not separate from each other in the bigger scheme (see Chapter 2), clutter of all kinds affects our spaces and our lives, even if it's not ours. So, next time you're in the checkout line, or library, or bank, or airport, become aware of how you're feeling. If a physical or emotional squall hits you suddenly, like a headache, or a heaviness in the chest, or a sad thought, it is most likely not yours! Feel the feeling without identifying it as yours, and *move on*!

Be mindful of what you take with you or leave behind in the form of energy droppings. The less identified you can be around any weather you encounter, the easier it will be to call back what is yours, let go what is not yours, and snip away the energetic ties or strings. Responding consciously means taking response-ability.

This is conscious clearing at a very high level and can begin with clearing out a single drawer.

The six practice stages beginning in Chapter 4 are designed specifically to guide you to living, and clearing, consciously.

String Cleaning

The first time I space-cleared my own home, I discovered to my horror that I was a clutterholic of the silent and hiding kind. My house had always been neat as a pin, organized, AND jammed beyond capacity with stuff. For all of you out there who think us "tidy types" are some kind of superhuman *wunderkind*, you may be relieved to know that being organized and being clear are not always the same, at least not in my case. It was time for me to look at my own stuff and the reasons behind my toxic squirrel tendencies.

One fall weekend, my husband and I had the brilliant idea of pulling down all the boxes containing twenty years of our respective professional lives. For me it was boxes and boxes of every quiz, test, paper topic, and syllabus that I had ever assigned to my high school students. I had even saved copies of these "just in case" I needed the extra set. I had assignments that had been mimeographed with purple ink, typed on a standard typewriter, and stuck together with rusty old paper clips. The hundreds of these paper clips looked like a small mountain when I finished! The amount of stuff I had saved was staggering, dating back to 1976 when I began my teaching career.

It took all afternoon and the next afternoon as well. Boxes and bags of paper began to line our sidewalk for the recycling truck that comes by each week. My entire career went into those bags.

When the recycling truck came around a few days later I watched as the Trash God lifted each and every sack. I put my shaky hands together in a prayerful gesture of gratitude and blessing as I watched the entire contents of my former life depart forever. I didn't know about strings back then. I just felt light beyond words! I floated for days afterwards.

A few hours had passed when I ran into an acquaintance who mentioned casually that she was selling her small upright piano. She wanted to move it fast so she was offering it at a good price. Hmmm. A piano. My wheels began to turn. So this is what it means to make space. Sometimes we don't know what we're making room for and it can be interesting to see what shows up when you're not expecting anything. I didn't really know it at the time, but we had just created space for music to come into our lives. We had also created space for new friendships. The people who sold us the piano have since become some of our dearest friends.

The Ripple Effect

I often hear stories from my clients and students that the biggest clutter clearing challenge is not the clearing part *per se*. Their biggest problem is getting their partner, kids, family members, or even neighbors to clear their own ****!?/@##*&!**** mess!

No question that a daily dose of tripping over sneakers, newspapers, hampers of unfolded laundry, dogs' toys, piles of this and that … is enough to make anyone feel defeated from the get-go. We can lead a horse to the proverbial clearing well, but in the end, we can't force it to do a thing with it. And because there is no such thing as separation in the bigger scheme, for better or worse, their clutter is our clutter.

The good news is that as we embark on our *own* clearing journey, we are creating significant energetic openings. Though the effect is subtle, the Law of Attraction ensures that these openings can create a powerful ripple effect to attract more possibilities for clearing.

When we harp on our beloved family members for being slobs, we are creating a second type of ripple effect. Our endless pestering creates a ripple effect of divisiveness and polarization, feeding old patterns that bring about more stubborn defensiveness. When has haranguing ever delivered the goods?

When I began my clearing journey, I cleared out only that which belonged to me. I focused on things I no longer loved or needed: *my* books, my clothes, my professional materials (and paper clips), my memorabilia, and any household items that I considered mine by eminent domain. The more I cleared, the easier it got, and the lighter I felt. In fact, I actually lost ten pounds in no time flat without any change to my diet. And my family members? I let them stew in their own juices. I insisted they contain their stuff and gently suggested that any stray articles found in common areas would be seized.

My daughter had grown to be quite the little squirrel at the ripe old age of eight and her room had become a rat's den of beloved treasures. One day, quite out of the blue, she announced that she was ready to part with of a closet full of Barbie dolls and Beanie Babies, doll clothes, "baby" books, and many toys of all shapes and sizes. I couldn't believe my ears!

Together we cleared. We set things aside for the yard sale, the Goodwill, the trash. She was so laser-like in her clearing and intentional in her mission that it took my breath away. I especially loved it when she would take me to task for holding back an item or two that was too good or too precious to give up.

How did my daughter suddenly get so determined about her clutter clearing? I didn't realize it at the time, but she had not only absorbed my new habits of clearing, she had also become a pro in much less time, and with a lot less messy, stringy, and heavy-hearted attachments.

My husband, in his own measured way, joined the clearing club as well. I love that he now gets bothered when he sees certain things out of place, like dishes that have not been washed or put away. I couldn't have orchestrated the changes that ensued with my family members if I'd offered them each a million bucks.

Clearing begets more clearing. Moving energy creates more energy. It's that simple. What, how much, and when, is not important. The point is, the less attached we can be to the outcome of our efforts, the more spaciousness we create at every level. So here's my advice:

- Focus on clearing your own "mess."
- Let go of attachment to clearing other people's messes.
- Let the ripple effect work its magic.

You Can't Take it With You, or Can You?

It's pretty obvious that we cannot take our savings account with us when we die. No pearl necklaces, no photo albums, no sports car ... But who is to say that we don't carry our best (and worst) memories, passions, and attachments, in the form of energy, with us to the next dimension when we pass on? Aren't we energy beings, after all? What this suggests is that all those invisible patterns and strings mentioned earlier get to come along for the ride. And if there is such a thing as reincarnation, it would mean that these same strings would come along for the next round, and the next, piling on like wet, stinky blankets that obscure our view and our vision of who we really are.

As a space clearing professional (see Preface), I am trained to feel the residue of invisible energy patterns left behind by previous occupants in a home or workplace. I can feel the heavy stickiness of human emotions anchored in places, the energetic force-fiields which cause the current occupants to wonder why they can't sleep, or why they're depressed or sad all the time, or broke. The negative charge held in the space links the space to the person who left it there until it is cleared, even if the person has already died! So when you think of ghosts, they are not really people who are stalking the householders, but rather, highly-charged negative thought patterns or memories left behind by someone who was having a hard life. *Read*: highly charged droppings.

To illustrate how clearing spaces clears previous occupants, I'll share something interesting that happened to me after I space-cleared my house for the first time. A day or two after the clearing, I happened to receive a call from someone I had known casually for several years from my yoga class. "You're not going to believe this, Stephanie," she said, almost out of breath, "but the house you live in was my house for fourteen years!" My friend was looking for my phone number in the directory and was stunned to see *her* old address pop up under my name! She had raised her three kids in this house. The red enamel wood-burning stove we now use every winter was the same one she had had installed. The tulips and the peonies that we enjoy every spring were her gifts to the place.

What I learned during our conversation was that my friend had suffered an unexplainable stomach ailment and intense release on the very day that I had cleared the house. It's impossible to say for sure, but the mysterious weather that moved through her rather suddenly could have been the result of a conscious cleansing of my home.

Whatever your belief in the invisible or in the hereafter may be, remember that our negative stress and holding patterns could be stuck somewhere else and/or still go with us even when we die. What better reason to clear, clear, clear, right now, while we are able to lighten our load and make a difference. When we release our strings and droppings by acknowledging our feelings and detaching from their drama and stickiness, we make it possible to move on—or pass over—with a cleaner slate. And everyone wins!

Water as a Mirror

If everything you've just read still doesn't convince you of the power you have to change your life, then consider the work of the Japanese scientist, Dr. Masaru Emoto. He provides some of the most compelling evidence of the power of the mind to affect reality.

Using high-speed photography, Dr. Masaru Emoto has developed a way to photograph the crystals of frozen water from many different sources. He takes water samples from sacred areas and polluted areas; natural water and tap water; water that has been prayed upon, reviled, and ignored; glasses of water shown the words "Love and Gratitude," and "You fool;" water that has been played classical, jazz, and heavy metal music; water before an earthquake and after, and so on.

What he's discovered is that the integrity of the crystal shapes of his "subjects" varies in proportion to the level of consciousness held by them. Frozen water crystals from a pure, clean, mountain lake that has been prayed over, for instance, take on an exquisite, hexagonal crystal shape. The photographs of these crystals look like gorgeous sparkling jewels and are enough to make your heart sing with joy when you look at them.

Crystals from polluted or neglected water sources, on the other hand, have no shape at all or are hideously deformed. Glasses of water that have been shown words like "Satan," "Hitler," or "You fool!" also have no shape at all or, as in the case of "You make me sick, I will kill you" (in Japanese), remarkably display an image of a man with a gun. The photographs of these crystals are painful to look at and are enough make your heart sink (sick).

The crystals visibly demonstrate how the higher vibrational frequencies of love and gratitude are more coherent than lower frequencies of hate and pain. Though Dr. Emoto has found that these shapes—or no shapes—will vary somewhat according to the language spoken or written, they essentially maintain a consistency that is universal to all of them. The most stunningly beautiful of them all, according to Emoto, is the water crystal that has been shown the words "Gratitude and Love" in any language!

Because of water's natural ability to "copy and memorize information," it is the perfect vehicle for studying the effects that thoughts and words have on people, places, and things. In his book *The Hidden Messages in Water* he says:

> "The written words themselves actually emit a unique vibration that the water is capable of sensing. Water faithfully mirrors all the vibrations created in the world, and changes these vibrations into form that can be seen with the human eye."[12]

So, if you ever doubted the power that your words have on you, your life experience, and on others, think again! Imagine what just reading the words in this book can do to begin to lighten your load; to soften your beliefs, and change your concepts of clutter and clearing—even if you don't believe them totally. You certainly have nothing to lose by trying.

Below you have an opportunity to play with these concepts, to see things as energy, and to notice your thoughts and feelings as you do so.

♏ Tune In: Sensing Energy

When we live our lives on automatic pilot we lose touch with the things and activities that make our hearts sing, and cringe. Here's an opportunity to tune in to a sampling of sensory experiences and see what "vibe" you get. Remember that there is no right or wrong, good or bad, answer to any of these. Someone's perception and experience of harmony could be someone else's perception and experience of pain. The bottom line is that you have a tangible experience of coherent and incoherent patterns of energy—both valuable teachers that can help you make more informed choices in your life.

Again as before, there is nothing to "do" with these simple exercises. Just allow your senses to speak for themselves and shed light for you. Be your own silent witness.

❑   Take one small object that you love (*read*: love madly, adore, makes your heart sing!) and one small object that you do not love or use (aka clutter). Place the object of clutter behind you and hold the object you love in front of you. Fully "be" with the object you love using all of your senses. What is the vibe you get? Notice your body as it holds this object. Notice your thoughts and beliefs about this object without identifying with them. What information can you glean from just being with this? When you feel complete, place the object you love behind you and bring forward the object of clutter. Repeat the above sensing exercise. When you have completed this task, place both objects side by side in front of you. Can you feel the energetic difference between the two as you sense one and then the other? Record all sensations in your clearing journal.

❑ Eat one food item that nourishes you completely and makes you swoon and one food item that has no nutritional or taste value whatsoever. Sense their energetic effects on your body. How do you feel while eating them and then several hours afterwards? As in the previous exercise, experience them separately and record your impressions (physical, mental, emotional) in your journal.

❑ Spend a day wearing clothes that you love—that fit and flatter you and make you feel good. Spend another day wearing something that doesn't fit, feel right, or look good. How do each of these make you feel? Notice what you attract to yourself in each case. How do others respond to you in each instance? Compare these two experiences and record your impressions (physical, mental, emotional) in your journal.

❑ Read or look at something that inspires and uplifts you and makes your heart sing. This can be a book or magazine, pictures or words. Repeat this with junk material that has no redeeming value to you, be it because it's dull, sensational, or scary. Compare these two experiences and record your impressions (physical, mental, emotional) in your journal.

❑ Smell an object that is sweet, pleasant, and uplifting and an object that makes you recoil. Fresh lemon wedges or lavender sachets opposite just-worn soccer cleats come to mind. Compare these two experiences and record your impressions (physical, mental, emotional) in your journal.

❑ Listen to a piece of music that is uplifting and makes your heart sing and a piece of music that feels intrusive or intense or chaotic. Notice what your body does when it hears harmonic patterns that you love and dissonant patterns that are unpleasant. Compare these two experiences and record your impressions (physical, mental, emotional) in your journal.

❑ Watch a show on television that inspires you, uplifts you or makes you laugh out loud one day. Repeat with a show that dumbs you down, scares you, or numbs you out, on a different day. Notice your body and feelings during the show and for an hour afterwards in each instance. Compare these two experiences and record your impressions (physical, mental, emotional) in your journal.

❑ Spend an hour in a space that is beautiful, harmonious, and clutter-free. Repeat by spending an hour in a space that is cluttered. Try to be as mindful of your sensate and energy body as possible. How do you feel during and afterwards? Compare these two experiences and record your impressions (physical, mental, emotional) in your journal.

* * *

Summary: Clutter as Energy

- Energy is a wave pattern that forms, un-forms, and informs.
- Physical objects are a collection of atomic and sub-atomic particles with a frequency and intensity.
- Energy holds no grudges; it doesn't care if you're having a bad day.
- The energy of clutter is denser, less coherent, and vibrates at fewer cycles per second than the energy of things we love.
- Most of the stress you feel is not yours; it becomes "yours" the moment you identify with it.
- You attract at the level that you vibrate.
- *Strings* are sticky energetic attachments that bind people and things to each other; they go with us everywhere we go, and will increase in number until they are cleared.
- *Droppings* are highly charged stress patterns that stick to the environment; they have a strong magnetic field and attract more of themselves if not cleared.
- You clear strings and droppings principally by feeling their charge with no attachment.

Part II

The Journey of Clearing

♋

We do not have to improve ourselves,
we just have to let go of what blocks our heart.
—Jack Kornfield

Chapter Four

Feel to Heal

All great discoveries are made by those whose feelings
run ahead of their thinking.
—C.H. Parkhurst

About the Journey

In the previous three chapters we explored some of the ways that clutter shows up in our lives and blocks our true nature. Hopefully these introductory chapters and the Tune In practice exercises have given you a glimpse of the bigger picture and a taste of what is possible.

The next six chapters (4-9) will guide you to clear slowly and sustainably—in stages. The six-stage sequence is designed specifically to help you bypass the brain and body's natural tendency to go into unconscious reaction (and contraction) whenever you step out of your comfort zone to clear. Taking the slow boat and the longer view by following the gentle progression outlined in Part II may not feel as satisfying in the short run, but when applied consistently over time, this program has the staying power to create a sea change of global proportions.

In this chapter, we will focus on the concept of feeling as a principal means for clearing. Specifically, we'll explore some of the ways we can bypass the noise and weather that our clutter dishes out (via the mind) in order to access information that is pure and clear and reliable. You will have the opportunity to experience how the body, the most powerful sensing tool available to us, is one of the best conduits of clear information that we have at our disposal.

As you open yourself to feel again as part of the clearing practice, it is possible you might encounter some interesting terrain. Let's first take a look at the signposts you could expect to find along the path to clarity, which, I cannot repeat often enough, *are a normal part of the journey.*

Signposts of Clutter Clearing

It's natural human behavior to seek immediate gratification for our efforts. Our hope is to feel lighter (more at ease, balanced, comfortable, peaceful, enriched, in the flow ...) after a few hours or a weekend wrangling our stuff into boxes and trash bags. But because most of us are looking at a lifetime of holding patterns, it can take some time for the "softening tools" to produce their desired effect. Lifting the lid on some deeply-held attachments can bring up even more weather and throw us off course if we're not paying attention.

When you clear using the exercises in this book, you will be putting into motion some powerful intentions. No matter how miniscule your clearing efforts and goals may seem, it's important to remember that clearing even just one toothpick will create an opening into spaciousness.

The four markers described below will help you recognize some of the natural phases that spring up as a result of a daily practice in clearing. They'll help you recognize that something might in fact be shifting for you, even if changes are too subtle to notice or the outcomes are not exactly what you were expecting. Here are the signposts; think of them as little "weather advisories" to carry along with you:

1. Feelings come up—*allow* them.
2. Shift happens—*embrace* it.
3. Outcomes change—*accept* them.
4. Clarity comes into focus—*trust* it.

Here's what they mean:

Feelings Come Up—Allow Them

By definition, clutter clearing releases energy that has been stuck for a long time, sometimes for an entire lifetime. When energy is moved in a big way, it is possible to feel more tired than usual or more cranky and edgy or uncomfortable. You may feel more emotional, or have a bout of panic or grief, anger or sadness. You may notice yourself shutting down completely. You may experience spaciness, memory lapses or mental fog, or the opposite, feeling more alive, energized, excited, and clear!

You may yawn more than usual, or tear, or burp, or fart, or feel nauseous. You may get unexplainable physical symptoms like headaches or backaches. You may sleep more, or you may have too much energy to sleep. You may want to quit. You may feel more out of control or desperate to escape with cravings for food, alcohol, TV, exercise. You may feel awesome one moment, and completely fall apart the next—all in less than sixty seconds!

If you want to put someone to sleep, start talking about your clutter. This, in fact, is what happens in my workshops when people begin to shed light on the places that they have held in the dark for so long. The entire room begins to look like the poppy fields in the *Wizard of Oz*!

Symptoms of clearing are the myriad ways that the body processes old stuff (as information) that is coming to the surface. They are signs of detoxification that result from raising the energetic frequencies in our home and in our life. They are ways the ego copes with the idea of letting go and feeling those feelings. They are the result of expansion energies colliding with contraction energies—no different than a high-pressure system slamming into the sluggish low-pressure holding patterns. Storms come up naturally. Don't be too hard on yourself.

Shift Happens—Embrace It

One of my favorite quotes is by Ram Dass, who acknowledges what happens to us when our tightly-held self-concept begins to break apart: "There is a grief that occurs when who you thought you were starts to disappear." To those of you who feel that your very identity is deconstructing before your own eyes, take comfort and allow yourself to feel this loss. Letting go of heavy-duty holding patterns can feel like a death. Honor these phases, for it *is* a true dying of your former self as it makes room for something new.

Shifts can come in other forms, too. One stage in childbirth is called transition. This is when the mother is shifting from labor to pushing mode. It is typically the shortest and the most intense stage of the entire birth and a signpost that the end of labor is near. There are transition points in clearing, too, that take us to whole new levels of awareness within ourselves. There's no mistaking these. These are the times when clearing your clutter might result in a healing crisis or a crisis of confidence. You might lose your job or home or your partner of twenty-five years. You may feel totally alone or empty or disconnected from your life purpose. You may find yourself at the end of your rope, ready to throw in the towel, shouting obscenities at anything that moves. As George Leonard says in another one of my favorite quotations: "Your resistance to change is likely to reach its peak when significant change is imminent." Pay close attention to this marker. It may be a clue that something is about to shift for you in what could be a very BIG and positive way.

In the clearing journey, the universe has a way of giving us what we need, not always what we want. While the ego is concerned with our comfort, the soul doesn't care if we're comfortable or not. Its job is to help us evolve. If any of the big storms do try to knock you down, don't lose heart, and don't give up. Remember it is the nature of this stage to *not know*. Give yourself a lot of supporting self-care and trust that you will get through it! It is precisely at this stage that your holding patterns are losing their grip on you. You're about to see a whole other side to your being that's been hanging out there all along. No matter how bad it feels, I'm here to tell you: This is a very good sign! Congratulations!

Outcomes Change—Accept Them

You might also attract what I like to call freebies from the universe. Freebies are those divine nuisances that we get at the most inopportune moments. Usually unsolicited, they remind us to pay attention. They give us new opportunities to shift our perception and reframe our thoughts.

Delays in traffic, cancelled flights, missed appointments. These freebies are a much subtler version of a healing crisis. They are all those times we trip, or bonk our head, or stub our toe, or break our leg. They are when the toilet overflows, or the car runs out of gas, or we lose our date book or the computer crashes. Freebies often give us a clue that something we're doing is off and we're being nudged back on. Freebies can also be an indicator of something being very *right* for once. Not getting into the supposed "best" college, or losing the bid on a particular job or house you wanted, may be a blessing in disguise.

You can ask the universe to bring these freebies on gently, in ways that you will understand and easily integrate into your life. Use them to practice letting go. They are a great teacher.

Clarity Comes into Focus—Trust It

As you clear away the clutter of your life you become more aware of information coming through that feels true and right. This is powerful because in fact, it is pure, uncontaminated, and unfiltered information that is bypassing the rational, ego-driven, monkey mind. You may not be able to explain what is coming through, but some part of you just *knows*. Don't dismiss those little flutters of clarity. Don't deny those true feelings of inspiration that have a way of sneaking in the back door. It will **feel like** your radio signals are coming through with much less static. You **will see** things you hadn't seen before, and the world may look more sparkly and vibrant and alive to you.

Information may show up as an intuition to do or not do something. It may show up in a dream, or an opportunity, or a phone call, or a synchronicity. You may be thinking of someone that then just happens to show up in your life. It may be something that makes you laugh or makes you feel calm and unattached. If you pay close attention you may notice that what's bubbling up are the stirrings of your soul, your deepest yearnings, your highest wisdom—your true, most spacious self! Embrace and enjoy these moments. They are just the beginning.

The Body Knows

If you tried the sensing exercises in the previous chapter, you may have noticed that your body, with its extraordinary sensing capabilities of smell, touch, sight, sound, taste, and inner knowing, can be a key source to a wealth of information. Unfortunately, most of us tend to shut down or dismiss this amazing resource and rely mostly on the intellect to provide us with the vital information we need to carry us from day to day. Every time we second-guess ourselves, we are allowing the mind to call the shots … again.

If we consider that this "intelligence" comes through the murky lenses and filters of our past—our conditioning, our fears, our judgments, and our attachments—we can see how its reliability for delivering pure, clear information can be mighty questionable.

There is no better way to clear than to invite our thinking minds to step aside and allow our feelings to be our guide. Without the body we can't sniff out the places in our homes that are really stuck. Without the body, we can't sense a potentially harmful situation. Without the body, we can't experience the full effect of weather patterns to show us where we hold on. The thing about our body is that it has a way of sussing out holding patterns in an instant that the busy mind cannot even touch (literally).

While I was writing this chapter, someone came to my front door soliciting financial support for some rather hazy scholarship fund. The kid seemed friendly enough, shaking my hand and acting as if we were old friends. Deep down in my bones I *smelled* a scam. It was disarming that he knew my name and said that my neighbor had sent him. I managed to finesse a quick retreat and get back to my writing. I wouldn't have thought much of this encounter except that I felt really off-center, jangled and just plain icky. My normally positive frame of mind felt contaminated, somehow: opened up to a wave of intense weather that included a huge dose of unworthiness. My inner critic suddenly went on a wild spree of bashing everything: my book, my efforts, my life.

If I hadn't paid attention to the signals I was receiving from my body, the unnerving shock waves, and the ridiculous nonsense that my mind was spewing out, I might have allowed this one event to take over and ruin my day. I had enough presence of mind to recognize that the weather I was feeling, *was not mine*. I also had to smile at how the universe delivers me these "this is only a test" freebies just when I need to make a point! The point being of course, in case it's not yet immediately obvious: *We must feel in order to clear.*

Clearing is Feeling

It is important to clarify that "feeling" as a vehicle for clearing, is not the same as "emoting." Feeling is not an expressive act, but an ability to open up the channels that *allow* information—be it highly charged, or not—to simply pass through us.

Feeling requires a level of detachment. Though this may seem oddly paradoxical, what you will learn in the coming chapters is that there is a quality of witnessing in the feeling process that differs greatly from the more familiar emotional venting, or reacting. Feeling is a way that we respond to information from our environment.

Responding opens up our channels; reacting shuts them down.

So, when you are asked to "feel your feelings" as part of the clearing process, what it means exactly is this:

1. *Allow* any weather—be it stormy or clear—to pass through to the extent that you can handle it.
2. *Experience* this information through your physical and non-physical senses. If it's clammy hands, notice them. If it's resistance, experience it. If it's nausea, allow it. If it's tears, shed them. If it's shame, embrace it.
3. And finally (this is key), **don't identify**, own, or take any of it personally. Allow it to be a passage of weather as information and feedback, nothing more.

There is a wonderful book called *Ask and It Is Given: Learning to Manifest Your Desires*, by Esther and Jerry Hicks, that offers us a glimpse as to why we might want to choose to feel. The message of this book is not Esther's herself but that of a Spirit Guide named Abraham, who delivers his teachings through her when she is in a clear, meditative state. Abraham speaks to the issue of manifesting our deepest desires and suggests that the reason we don't get what we want in our lives is that our clutter patterns do not match our desire patterns. He says:

> "The reason you have not already gotten what you desire is because you are holding yourself in a vibrational holding pattern that does not match the vibration you desire. That is the only reason—ever! And the important thing for you to now understand is that if you will stop and think about it, or more important, stop and feel about it, you can identify your very discord."[13]

Abraham tells us that our feelings are the only true indicator of where we are open to our deepest yearnings and where we close down. Pure joy and effortless ease, for example, would be an indicator of complete alignment. Pure conflict and dis-ease, would not. Pretty simple, when you think about it. As he puts it:

> "The way you feel is a clear and accurate indication of your alignment, or misalignment with your Source Energy. In other words, your emotions let you know if you are allowing, or if you are in a current state of resistance to, your connection with Source."[14]

♏ *Try This: Feeling Check*

1. Put this book down and take a minute or two to notice how you are feeling at this very moment. What is your body sensing? Is there any weather coming up? What is going through your mind? Do you feel any tightness, contraction, or shortness of breath, for example? Do you feel any emotional weather like worry or fear or anxiety or boredom? Or mental weather, such as judgment or criticism? Are you yawning? Are you excited, or happy, or jazzed? Are you zoning out?

2. Next, re-read the Abraham quotations in the previous section. Notice what goes through your mind as you read them, and how you feel in your body. Do these quotes capture your imagination or inspire you? Are you trying too hard with your intellect to understand or analyze them? Perhaps your eyes bugged out and your mind did a double-take when you saw the words "Spirit Guide" above. If so, notice the charge that may be activated right now. If your inner critic piped in with an opinion or a judgment, consider this, too, as feedback of possible resistance.

3. Now read the paragraph and quotations again after naming your feelings and see if you notice a difference in yourself. Do the passages resonate differently? Do you glean something new by reading them a third time?

If, for the remainder of this book, you can allow yourself to make frequent "feeling checks" like this one—to stop, breathe, name, and feel whatever you're feeling in the moment—you will gain the true spirit of the clearing journey, called awareness! And also, believe it or not, you might even release loads of invisible clutter strings you're inadvertently attracting into your life and dragging around with you!

Adopt "stop and feel" as your best friend for the remainder of the book and you may notice some miraculous shifts taking place in your life.

Hanging Out In *Not Knowing*

Quitting the career and job that defined me for two decades (detailed in the Preface) led to a long period of fumbling in a foggy netherworld I call *not knowing.* I still find myself visiting that place from time to time. These moments come on when I might least expect them, and often when something new is about to be born. I never know how long these periods will last, but they have become like old friends that I do my best to welcome into my life.

A poem written by the famous German poet, Rainer Maria Rilke (when he was all of twenty-seven years old) sustains and inspires me whenever I find myself, yet again, hanging out in the fog. Written as a letter in 1903 to an aspiring young poet, the passage contains a universal truth that speaks volumes to all of us.

"Be patient towards all that's unsolved in your heart," it begins, gently urging us to live our questions "like locked rooms and like books that are written in a very foreign tongue." Rilke suggests that answers cannot be given to us because we "would not be able to live them." And "the point" he goes on to say, "is to live everything ... Live the questions now. Perhaps you will then gradually, without noticing it, live along some distant day into the answer."[15]

When we make space in our lives—by conscious choice or not—we are likely to enter a period of deep unknowing, where nothing we do or experience makes any sense in the context of what preceded it; where our vital connections seem completely lost. We may even hit the proverbial wall and splatter all over the floor, as I have done so many times in my life. Rilke's poem invites us to meet these periods in our lives with spaciousness, to accept not knowing as a legitimate state of being, to experience the mystery of these moments as little flower buds that cannot be rushed or forced or seen. Yet.

Allow the mystery. Feel its twists and turns and seeming dead-ends. This is a very juicy place in which to hang out if you can bear the uncertainty and discomfort of it. I have found these periods in my life to be powerful and creative—dark and messy and exasperating a lot of the time, but rich, like black soil that fosters new growth.

Following Your Knows

If you think about it, we humans are like radios that receive and transmit information, as energy, all the time. The body's sophisticated sensing capabilities are the antennae and processing center for all the signals we receive and send out. Sensations (called feelings in this book) give us the means to read and interpret these signals.

Though we can count on all of our senses to pick up information from our environment, many of us have one or two senses with which we tend to lead. For example, I have a highly developed sense of smell. I can smell things before I can see them. I can smell gas leaks that most might not. I can smell cigarette smoke from smokers in passing cars, even if their windows are rolled up! I can even smell stress patterns (droppings) that have been left behind by previous occupants in homes for decades! I can smell energetic "off-gassing" when I am clearing a person or being cleared.

As you embark on your clearing journey, accept your body as one of your most highly developed sources of undeniable information. Notice the ways that you typically tune in to receive, read, and transmit signals from your environment. Notice if you are more likely to get a visual image, or an auditory sound, or a kinesthetic knowing. Having this awareness can help you sniff out the places in your home that don't feel very good, or feel stuck. It can help you tune in to peoples' true motivations and assess whether they serve your highest good or not. Continued practice with the Tune In suggestions at the end of Chapter 3 can help you develop your awareness and sensing abilities even further.

Try this little acid test and see if it can help you identify one or several senses with which you might typically lead. When you're talking casually with someone, which of these phrases are you most likely to use?

- I *know* what you mean.
- I *see* what you mean.
- I *hear* what you're saying.
- I *sense* what you're saying.

- I'm *touched.*
- I can just *taste* it.
- I can *visualize* it.
- I can *smell* it a mile away.
- I *smell* trouble.
- I can just *imagine* that.

Mining for Answers

We cannot talk about our five senses in the context of clearing without also considering the crucial role of the sixth. Our sixth sense is the home of our gut instinct; the place in us that just knows. We usually can't explain how we know, or measure how we know, or even prove how we know something. We just know. In this more invisible realm we can only know by having a personal, direct experience. The problem that usually arises, of course, is that we're too cluttered to know that we know!

Belleruth Naparstek's description of our inner knowing is more elegant than mine. In her very readable and practical book *Your Sixth Sense,* she says:

"Because these occurrences seem to arrive unbidden and don't fit into our rationalist view of the world, we usually discount them or forget about them. But we're missing a big opportunity. Because with or without our conscious agreement, just below the surface of our lives, this boundless abiding intelligence quietly sits and waits for us to recognize it."[16]

Here's a quick and easy tool that I like to use when I'm too stuck in my head and I can't decide whether or not do something, or let something go. It allows me to tap into and act from the place that already knows:

- If it feels right, I do it.
- If it doesn't feel right, I don't do it.
- If I don't know, I wait until I know.

It may seem trivial but there is an infinite wisdom to this simple three-step process. For me, it's like using the writer's bump on my finger to figure out my left from my right, or spelling "WE" to locate East from West. When using this tool to make an assessment, I have found it helpful to click an imaginary "quit" button on my thinking self before opening the feeling function of my knowing self.

I've noticed that when I allow myself to back away from a dilemma or wait it out during those times of "I don't know," sometimes my quandary has a way of resolving all by itself. For example, I remember spending over an hour on the phone trying to sort out a fare impasse with a travel agent, which resulted in my being bounced around in circles from agent to agent, from voice mailbox to voice mailbox. Finally, nearly ready to bag an entire trip and erase all the progress I had made, I simply stopped trying. I hung up the phone with Agent Number Six and made dinner instead. I decided not to decide.

In spite of the control freak part of me who can't stand leaving things hanging unresolved for longer than a minute, I did the unthinkable and walked away. You can imagine my surprise when I received a call the next day from a very friendly customer service representative confirming an even better fare and schedule! Recognizing that I didn't have the means to change the outcome at a particular moment in time resulted in my ultimate success.

Instead of trying to push or force an answer, I might begin with just saying, "I don't know right now" and follow it up with a question. If it's a dilemma about what to order at a restaurant for example, I might ask my body, "What is it that would most nourish you right now?" or, "What food would make you feel really great for the rest of the day?" and allow the answer to bubble up. If it's a question about how to best use my time, I might ask myself, "Which task would help me feel most productive this morning?" If time is short and I'm feeling overwhelmed and stuck, I might ask, "What is one quick thing I can do that would help me feel lighter (clearer, calmer) right now?" I try to go for *the feeling of an outcome* as much as possible.

I might pose bigger life questions as queries or mystery questions to be cultivated and lived. As I'm going to bed, I'll ask my unconscious to give me a dream that is easy to remember the next morning. Sometimes my dreams or dream fragments come through symbolically like puzzle pieces that don't make any sense at first, taking several days or weeks to come into focus. My answers have a way of coming through in the most unusual and unexpected ways, so I do my best to pay attention to those small, whispery details.

Sometimes I can massage an answer if I need one right away. For instance, I notice when I take my usual walking route that there comes a point in one of the bends in the road where I might spontaneously receive some clarity about an issue that has eluded me all day. I have received some of my best book ideas and chapter titles in that one spot. It's happened so often that I now look forward to seeing what guidance might pop up there. For me to receive a clear answer, I have to make sure that the question I pose is also very clear.

There are other instances when I'm likely to be inspired. I get a lot of clarity when I'm waking up in the morning, in that dreamy state just before getting out of bed, or when I'm practicing my softening yoga poses (see Chapter 9). I'll clear many mental cobwebs when I'm meditating. I tend to get a lot of goodies when I'm soaking in a hot bath.

Notice if there are certain places or circumstances where you are more likely to get information, guidance, inspiration, or some kind of clear signal about your next steps. Try sensing when your higher self sends you a message and see if there is a pattern to it. If you're a visual kind of person, for instance, pay attention to the images that come through. If you're an auditory person, listen for words or pitch or cues. Does getting a clear signal depend on you moving your body, feeling rested, taking many breaks, letting go of attachment to a particular outcome? Are you going for a feeling that you wish to experience?

Tapping the Body's Guidance

If something deep in your bones doesn't feel right, it is probably wise to listen. The problem comes when our systems are so flooded with noise and overwhelmed by static that nothing we do yields any clarity. Here is a simple way to help you bypass the monkey mind. It's called muscle testing.

Based on the fundamental principle that the body knows what it needs and what's best for it, practitioners of Applied Kinesiology use muscle testing to make determinations about healing strategies or substances that will serve their client's interests for optimal health and well being. It was through muscle testing that my friend was able to determine which one of the many rubber wristbands her daughter was wearing to promote a myriad of good causes was giving her skin allergies. Once she took off the offending bracelet, her condition cleared immediately.

You can muscle test yourself when you are in need of an answer that might directly benefit or affect you. You can test whether or not something serves your best interests. The only caveat is this: The tool will not work if you are attached to a particular outcome. It's easy for our desires and preferences to cloud the signals that our body receives and gives. What you learn is that the body never lies. It simply can't. It's the troublesome mind that gums up the works.

♍ *Try This: Muscle Testing For Guidance*

- ❑ With your non-dominant hand, touch the tip of your thumb to the tip of your pinkie, and press them together in a tight lock.
- ❑ With your other hand take your thumb and forefinger, insert it into the circle and try to break the pinkie-thumb lock apart. This will give you an idea of the mechanics.

❑ To learn your own body's code, say quietly to your self, "Show me a 'yes'" while inserting your forefinger/thumb into the loop of your other hand.

❑ If the seal holds its tension, that will be the indicator of your true "yes." If it can easily be broken, then this latter will indicate your body's "yes" response.

❑ Repeat the exercise with the phrase "Show me a 'no'." You should get the opposite response to your "yes." For me, my true "yes" pinkie/thumb loop stays tight, and my "no" will not be able to hold. If yours is the opposite, then this is your particular code. There's no right or wrong answer here.

❑ You can test this pattern with other true/false statements that are clear and unequivocal: "I am female," "I live in Oakland," "My maiden name is Jones," "I was born in 1953." By now you should get a pretty good read on the way your body delivers its feedback.

❑ You can ask any yes/no question provided that you are not attached to the outcome and you keep your questions really clear. For example, "Should I take the workshop?" might give you a very different answer than if you asked, "Is it in order for me to take the 'Strategies for Business' workshop?" or "Is it in order for me to take the 'Strategies for Business' workshop this coming weekend?" You can fine-tune your query by asking additional questions like: "Would it serve my highest good to take the 'Strategies for Business' workshop?" "Would it be in my best interest to stay home this weekend? The key is to be as precise as you can be with your yes/no questions.

❑ *Note*: It will take some practice to get the hang of this process if you've never done it before. This is a powerful tool. Be respectful of the power of your body to *know* and deliver information and try to be as quiet and detached when you pose a question.

❑ ***Caution***: *DO NOT use this tool to make a major decision that could be potentially life-threatening. It is very difficult—almost impossible—not to be attached to an outcome when the health and safety of a person you know and love is at stake.*

ᔥ *Try This: Shedding Layers by Shedding Light*

In Part I you had an opportunity to Tune In to the different faces of clutter (as "imbalance," as "perception," as "energy"). Review the three Tune In lists again and zero in on one or several that either brought up some weather in the form of an emotional or negative charge, or were something with which you resonated and connected on a deeper level (a yearning). Some of the ways you'll know that something is being stirred up in you is if:

- A button gets pressed or you feel angry;
- You feel a pang—of sadness, grief, or fear;
- You feel rattled, jangled, unsteady, off-balance, or even ill;
- A light bulb goes off and you get an ah-ha;
- You feel jazzed or excited, expanded, and hopeful;
- You feel a stirring in your heart or soul, a longing.

If nothing pops up, you can muscle test for guidance: e.g. "Show me a yes if this is an issue that would serve my highest good to explore right now."

Once you've chosen your topic, write down in your journal anything that comes up. Free-associate. Do not concern yourself with grammar or punctuation. The point is simply to shed light on the places that you hold on and open the channels to your source of guidance and deeper wisdom. Practice this activity every day for a week or a month or longer. You can begin by choosing one item or issue and completing these phrases:

- I feel …
- I think that …
- I see that …
- I know that …
- I'm afraid that …
- I wonder about …
- I wish …

Example 1

Let's say that when you scanned the weather list in Chapter 1, the item that gave you a momentary pang when you read it was "loneliness." You might write the word at top of the page and explore what it brings up for you. Perhaps you feel deep sadness and recall how as a child you were dismissed all the time by your family or were teased by the kids in your neighborhood. Try to tune in specifically to how you feel in your body, what visual images it conjures, what goes through your mind. Explore why this issue is up for you right now and how it might relate to the clutter you have. Remember, none of it needs to make sense. The point is simply to stop and feel.

Example 2

Perhaps it was "This stuff needs me" in Chapter 2 that rattled you. You realize that this takes up a lot of your energy and it has become your *modus operandi* for holding on to stuff you don't need or use. Maybe you feel suddenly enraged that as the first-born you were the glue that held the entire family together. You notice that surrendering control is really hard for you. Explore what would happen if you let others "fail." What would be the worst thing that could happen? Write the phrase "This stuff needs me" at the top of the page and explore the weather it brings up: how your body feels, what's going through your mind, the images you get, the emotions you re-experience.

Example 3

Maybe it's a sensing exercise you did in Chapter 3 that elicits some interesting ah-has for you. You notice that when you choose to wear a rather unattractive outfit, it makes you feel small and insignificant. As you peel away more layers you notice that you kind of like feeling small so that you can recede in the background. You notice that it feels safer and more comfortable to hide behind the baggy shirts. If you tried wearing something you loved that made you stand out and be noticed, write about how this felt to you. Use your journal to explore the feelings and connections that you are making, perhaps for the first time.

* * *

Summary: Feel to Heal

- Clutter is not just something you can see.
- Thinking comes through the lenses and filters of perception; pure feeling does not.
- The body offers you the finest physical and non-physical capabilities to feel and receive guidance.
- You need to feel your holding patterns in order to clear them.
- Taking regular Feeling Checks helps you to become more aware.
- Not knowing is a legitimate and creative state of being.
- Muscle testing helps you bypass the monkey mind.
- The ego gives you what you want and the soul gives you what you need; the soul doesn't care if you're comfortable or not.
- Shift happens, but not always the way you expect.

① Clearing Practice ①
Feeling

Goals: The practice this week is intended to help you tune in and feel: to awaken your natural sensing abilities, and learn new ways to tap into your personal source of guidance and information.

Tasks: Complete the following and add more as time and energy permit:

1. **First:**
   - ❏ Get yourself a journal or a notebook that will become your clearing companion for the duration of the clearing program. Get one that makes your heart sing—you'll be seeing a lot of it over the course of the next six weeks to six months.
2. **Every day:**
   - ❏ Beginning first thing in the morning, follow the directions specified in *Try This: Feeling Check* and practice #1 several times a day, or whenever you think of it.
3. **Once this week:**
   - ❏ Feeling Check: Take a moment and notice what it *feels* like when you repeat this phrase silently to yourself without trying to do or fix anything:
     - o "I feel spacious."
   - ❏ Set aside at least thirty minutes and follow the directions specified in *Try This: Shedding Layers by Shedding Light.*
   - ❏ Record in your journal any feelings, shifts, synchronicities, dreams, or ah-has that you notice from practicing this week's tasks and from the clearing journey in general.
4. **End of the week or month:**
   - ❏ Read Chapter 5 if you feel complete and ready to move forward to the next stage of clearing.

① Clearing Circle ①
Stage One

Note to first-timers:

- The Clearing Circle offers a sample agenda for those of you wishing to share your experiences with others as part of an ongoing clearing discussion or support group.
- Consider starting the Circle with an introductory meeting, which is fully outlined in Chapter 10 (see Sample First Meeting—Organizing the Circle).

Circle Reminders:

- Make sure all participants have read Chapters 1-4, reviewed the section entitled Clearing Circle in Chapter 10, and had some time to complete the Clearing Practice: *Feeling.*
- Read aloud, clarify, and agree to follow the Circle Ground Rules listed in Chapter 10, making any necessary adjustments.
- Be mindful of the time and keep the Circle moving; talk of clutter has a way of putting people to sleep, especially if your group meets in the evenings.
- Choose one person to facilitate the gathering.
- If you're flexible and not locked into a six-session program, consider spending more than one meeting on this first stage. There are plenty of topics here to generate several lively discussions. Better to take your time than to rush the group trying to cram it all in to one session.
- Remember, silence creates openings; don't be afraid of it.
- Start and end on time.

Circle Discussion: Complete the following and add more as time and energy permit:

1. Begin: [First meeting only].
- ❏ Share your name, why you're here, and how you hope to benefit from being in this group. *Note*: for step-by-step instructions see Sample First Meeting—Organizing the Circle in Chapter 10.

2. **Describe:**
   - ❏ What "spaciousness" means to you, how it manifests in your life, and what it feels like.
3. **Share:**
   - ❏ How your body gives you feedback; which of your six senses you tend to use the most;
   - ❏ Some of the ways you tap your intuition or source of inner guidance; how you know if the signals you're getting are true and reliable;
   - ❏ What it feels like to hang out in not knowing.
4. **Discuss Themes:**
   - ❏ Use the Summary highlights in this chapter to guide your discussion further (time permitting).
5. **Plan next meeting:**
   - ❏ Logistics, time, and place.

Chapter Five

Shift the Focus

When you change the way you look at things,
the things you look at change.
—Wayne Dyer

Where the Mind Goes, Energy Flows

The mind is like a toddler with a short attention span who goes after anything interesting and reachable. After a few minutes, he's bored and goes on to the next thing. Without his parents' constant attention, a toddler will go after stuff that isn't exactly in his highest interest—the kitchen knife, ongoing traffic, the *Drano* under the bathroom sink. Similarly, without the quality of mindfulness, our thoughts can easily turn to negative images, doom and gloom predictions, judgments, gossip, endless chatter ...

It's easy to "go there" when the trails that weave through our inner landscape are as well worn with fear as they are. Judging others and not taking responsibility can feel really good. Gossip is a culturally supported activity. Playing victim can lead to huge payoffs of attention from others in the short run. Fear is a slippery slope of self-fulfilling prophecies. Let the toddler mind go the way of fear and crawling back to neutral is a major hike.

Living and clearing consciously means pulling the toddler back *every* time he goes off on another one of his many excursions. Be it a tailspin of worry or self-doubt, our job is to reel in the strings and re-send them in a new, more positive direction.

Again and again and again.

In this chapter we will see how this super-elastic thing we call the mind can be a powerful vehicle for our purposes in clearing clutter. Like a toddler, the mind is actually relatively easy to re-direct if we're willing to mind it and not confuse it with mixed messages. The "kid" might throw some tantrums, but with practice and patience, he's capable of blazing new trails that are infinitely more joyous, uncomplicated, and clear.

Clearing with Intention

Clearing with intention is a way to get our higher self to communicate with the toddler mind, continuously steering her or him in the direction of our heart's longing. As we saw with Dr. Emoto's water studies in Chapter 2, thoughts and words alone have the power to change the course of reality. If attaching a piece of paper with the words "Love and Gratitude" to a glass of water can raise the vibration of the water, imagine what we can do with our minds to clear and raise the energy of our homes, relationships, and lives.

But clearing with intention is more than simply directing, or guiding our thoughts purposefully. Abraham, in the book *Ask and It Is Given*, suggests that we connect with the *feeling* of the thought in order to manifest at a level of our deepest yearnings:

> "… it is not so much about guiding your thoughts as it is about reaching for a feeling, because reaching for the way you would like to feel is an easier way to hold your thoughts in vibrational alignment with that which you believe is good."[17]

As the full-throttle engine of a powerful manifesting machine, our intentions cannot be understated. There are two caveats, however:

1. ***Be clear how you state, invoke, visualize, and feel your intentions.*** The engine, once fired up, will produce results! If you are visualizing and feeling more financial abundance in your life that is encoded with a sense of optimism, possibility, and expansiveness, the universe will respond in kind. If, on the other hand, you are sending a signal for more abundance, which is laced with worry, scarcity, or neediness, the universe *will respond to the scarcity signals* by giving you more scarcity. In short, it is the quality of feeling that you send out which delivers what you get.

2. ***Let go of attachment to the outcome.*** Results don't always come in the package or form that you might expect. By holding tightly to an agenda, an expectation, or a timetable, you close doorways that could lead you to places you never imagined. Your sole job here is to express (feel) your intention and get out of the way!

Envisioning "As if"

Feeling goes a long way to fire up the engine that will lead you to a more spacious life. But if you just can't bring yourself to feel or believe that you'll ever get there, or move the mountain that is your clutter, you can begin by just faking it. Pretend that your life is flowing and clear. Act as if you have already achieved your life purpose and deepest longing.

If your heart's desire is to live in a clear, clean, peaceful home, surrounded with nothing but beautiful plants, you can begin by cutting out pictures of magazines that reflect that spacious quality. You can bring home fresh flowers or a plant to remind you. If you yearn for a life partner, you can begin by envisioning this person and maybe even emptying out a drawer or two, or buying an extra toothbrush to attract this possibility. If you've been longing to get pregnant, imagine yourself already six months pregnant by spending a day with a pillow under your blouse and acting as if you already were. You can do it when nobody is around to think or tell you that you're being foolish.

Creating an image of what you want your life to look and feel like before, during, or after you have cleared your clutter is a powerful message to send to the unconscious mind. Remember, the unconscious doesn't know the difference between reality and the ideal image. By surrounding yourself with the energetic signature of these images, the unconscious will begin to organize a whole new reality based on these powerful intentions. It is doing so right now, in fact, just by reading these words!

After our daughter was born and it was clear that we had outgrown our cozy home in the city, my husband and I began the process of looking for a new place in a quieter, less urban community. We had no idea where the search would land us. For fun, we would take weekend drives into neighborhoods we loved even if they were out of state or out of our price range. We would photograph Victorian homes on quiet tree-lined streets because these captured the essence of what we loved most and dreamed about living in one day. The photos would then go into our "ideal image" album. Without getting too attached to the neighborhoods or falling into deep funks because we knew that most of these places were out of our reach, we simply allowed ourselves to enjoy and act as if. I would imagine my car in the driveway. I would pick the window that was our bedroom. I would consider the colors I might choose to repaint the facade.

After a couple of years passed, we were invited one day to have lunch at the home of a friend about twenty miles west of us. Her house was in a small town we had not considered before and knew almost nothing about. The streets, lined with mature oak and maple trees and graceful century-old Victorian homes, were spacious and welcoming. The houses looked almost identical to a neighborhood we had photographed in a whole other state two years before! There was even a "For Sale" sign that caught our eye on the front lawn of a cute house that turned out to be within our price range. On that day, we realized this town was a real possibility for us. Within about six months we found ourselves living in one of those houses that a few years prior we could only dream about. It was clear to us that we had manifested this place by holding a strong intention for what we wanted and a vision for what could be.

♍ Try This: Playing As If

Re-creating a more spacious vision for yourself is like developing a new muscle. Because positive images alone hold a very high vibration, they become very attractive and a powerful reminder of what is possible. It's also a lot of fun to pretend you have already manifested your deepest dreams. Remember that by focusing on the absence of a quality (i.e. the fear of not getting it, or the reasons why it might not come to pass) is equally effective for delivering results, so try to relax the fearful mind as much as possible. You can stay positive and focused by bringing to consciousness only that which you desire, and by reining in the toddler mind when it goes off again in the opposite direction.

Here are some ways to practice flexing this muscle:

❑ Place photos of your heart's desires in locations where you are likely to see them a lot: your screensaver, refrigerator, car. Replace or change the images when you feel that they have gone stale, or you no longer notice them.

❑ Create a collage or poster of all the images or words that express a quality of feeling you have been longing for: e.g. health and wellness, fitness, ideal weight, financial abundance, the perfect job, the perfect mate, financial security, a book contract, etc.

❑ Photograph peoples' homes, streets, yards, babies, cars, etc. and put them in an "ideal image album."

- Display a photo of someone who has defied huge odds to reach unimaginable heights of success and personal power like Nelson Mandela, Lance Armstrong, Maya Angelou.
- Write down this quotation and place it in a prominent place: "Work like you don't need money, love like you've never been hurt, and dance like no one is watching." (It's called "The Daffodil Principle"; I received it in an anonymous e-mail.)
- Put a photograph of your house you are trying to sell with a big "Sold" sign across the front and display it prominently. You can add "Sold for Asking Price" at the bottom if you wish.
- Bring the quality of natural sunlight into your home by placing full-spectrum light bulbs in your lamps and light fixtures (available at any natural foods store).
- Create a beautiful altar that anchors an intention and supports letting go.
- Get one hundred one-dollar bills out of the bank and scatter them all over the floor or bed and throw them up in the air as if you just hit the jackpot.
- Write yourself a check for a million bucks and display it so that it is the first thing you see when you wake up in the morning.
- Empty a drawer, buy a toothbrush, make a second set of keys to attract your life partner.
- Create a business card logo and tagline that expresses how you wish to be identified and reflects an aspiring "new you."
- Use your imagination to envision the life you desire, and enliven the life you already have. Remember to keep it fun and let go of your attachment to the outcome!

The Power of Ritual

If you think of dreams as the way that your unconscious mind communicates to you in special symbolic code while you sleep, ritual is one way you can consciously communicate back to your unconscious while you're awake. To the unconscious mind, "real live action" and "conscious intentional ritual" *are the same thing*! By creating a ritual of letting go, for instance, you can send a powerful message to your subconscious that letting go of clutter is doable and even fun.

Ritual is a great way to anchor your intentions. It helps you to massage and soften and release tough holding patterns and bring to conscious reality the longings of your heart. As Robert A. Johnson says in his book, *Owning Your Own Shadow*:

"You can draw it, sculpt it, write a vivid story about it, dance it, burn something, or bury it—anything that gives expression to that material without doing damage ... Remember, a symbolic or ceremonial experience is real and affects one as much as an actual event."[18]

♍ *Try These: Simple Rituals for Clearing and Letting Go*

❑ In the spirit of this Japanese saying, "Let the past drift away in the water," wash your hands slowly and mindfully after each phase of your day to create new energy and release the strings or attachments to the past.

❑ Repeat to yourself, "It's not mine," whenever you feel some weather creeping up suddenly, and imagine it blowing (peeling, falling, melting) away.

❑ After a bath: Imagine the draining water taking away old energy, thoughts, and beliefs.

❑ Burn incense and/or clap, rattle and bell to clear away something old or prepare a space for something new.

❑ Release by burning photos, letters, or thoughts written down on paper—with gratitude.

❑ Amplify your drinking water by placing the words "Gratitude and Love" on your glass or on the jug, facing inward.

❑ Amp up your food with your thoughts of praise, gratitude, and love.

❑ Visualize stuck energy moving out through your feet into the earth.

❑ Place a thought-form of a person, thing, belief, or issue you would like to release on the palm of your hand. Wish it Godspeed and blow it into the wind, with gratitude.

❑ Imagine cutting away any strings that you are still carrying by taking a few swipes all around you with your imaginary clearing sword—expressing gratitude as you do so.

❑ Write a letter to someone as if you were going to send it, but instead bless it and burn it with gratitude.

❑ Create an altar to a food item (a thing, a belief, an issue) with which you would like to change your relationship.

❑ At bedtime, let go of the busy-ness of your day by recalling everything that happened—from your most recent moment (getting into bed) to the first thing you can remember doing earlier that day (like getting out of bed). Unwinding your day in this manner creates space for you to sleep better and dream more vividly. I'm usually sound asleep by the time I try to remember what I had for lunch.

❑ Practice any Softening Attitude described later in this chapter.

❑ Create a special ritual of letting go using one object that symbolizes your holding patterns. Place it on a special altar to anchor your intentions (see next section). Wish it Godspeed and release it—with gratitude.

The Magic of Altars

Though we mostly associate these with churches or temples, the truth is altars can be found everywhere. If you really stop to think about it, the special flower centerpiece on a Thanksgiving table and the "good china" place settings are a kind of altar. They honor the circle of family and friends coming together once a year to give thanks. The photos on the bureau, the grouping of rocks and shells from a favorite beach or summer experience, the antique clock holding court on the mantel, the wreaths we hang to celebrate the seasons are just some of the ways we remember and connect with something timeless, something larger than ourselves.

One of my favorite celebrations in Mexico is called Day of the Dead (*Dia de los Muertos*). On November 1 and 2, when it is believed that the veil that separates the living from the dead is at its thinnest, people from all walks of life will gather around their homemade altars to remember and honor their dearly departed. Far from morbid, these occasions are festive and colorful, and generally last most of the day and night. Favorite foods and drinks of the deceased, flowers, candles, photographs, are placed on a special altar that can be as big and elaborate as to take up the entire living area of the home.

Altars offer us a direct connection to spirit and are a means through which we can experience our most spacious selves. They help us anchor our intentions, feel our deepest yearnings, quiet our mind, express gratitude, remember and pray for a loved one, feed our soul. Creating this spiritual focal point in our homes is easy, too. All you need is a table, a shelf, or a nook, somewhere in your house, apartment, or office. The rest is up to your imagination.

℞ *Try This: Altar of Letting Go*

Here's a simple way to create an altar dedicated to letting go of attachments of any kind:

❑ Find a small table, or a shelf, in a quiet place in your home where you can imagine spending at least a moment or two every day.

❑ In the spirit of the Japanese saying, "Let the past drift away in the water," consider adding a water element in the form of a symbol or a small fountain.

❑ On a colorful cloth that you love, place objects that make your heart sing.

❑ Add objects that represent things, people, beliefs, or outcomes you wish to release, e.g. books, clothing, photo of ex-husband or wife.

❑ Place and light a stick of incense if you wish. Sandalwood incense, called *Nag Champa*, is my favorite because it's pure and not overpowering.

❑ Place and light a candle and take a moment to connect in.

❑ Call in that which represents the Divine, or invite your higher self, to assist you in releasing the charge you are holding, and/or the strings that bind you to this thing, relationship, or issue. Ask for assistance in letting go of attachment to the outcome. Ask for support in creating openings that will help you access your higher wisdom and deeper yearnings.

❑ Additionally or alternatively: You can repeat any set of Softening Attitudes described later in this chapter.

❑ Stop and feel. Notice and allow any weather to move through.

❑ Remember to keep your altar fresh and vibrant. Change the objects when you feel them getting stale. Dust and clean regularly. Move the altar to another location if it's not working for you. Housing an altar that you are not using becomes another form of clutter!

The Miracle of Gratitude

It may be true that there is no such thing as a quick fix in this clearing adventure, but if I've learned anything at all, it is that being grateful for everything, all the time, can change the vibration of clutter and produce miracles! Expressing gratitude is pure gold for how it can change our life on a dime.

Don't take my word for it. Try it. Make a list of the things that might give you pause or make you groan or recoil. Perhaps it's the case of adult-onset acne, or the bills that keep piling up, the neighbor who plays her music too loud, or the army of ants that invade your kitchen every spring. Express your appreciation for these things in your life. Welcome them like old friends.

See if by shifting the focus, you notice something you hadn't noticed before. For example, when I began to name all the ants in my kitchen Beto (for no particular reason other than I liked that name and it rhymed with *vete* which means "go away" in Spanish), I began to have a different relationship with them. They didn't bug me so much anymore, and, believe it or not, they stopped coming in droves. Now I notice that only about one or two Betos appear around the kitchen sink to say hello on any given day.

I notice that if I extend a kind greeting to a telemarketer instead of hanging up on him or her, then I don't feel so jangled afterwards. I have also noticed that these calls have all but stopped! So have the store catalogues that used inundate our mailbox. When we release the charge we hold around certain people, things, or issues, they fall away.

Giving thanks has a way of magically reducing the charge we hold around things and people. It stops the endless cycle of negativity and releases the offending string. Putting a positive spin on everything may be cause for incessant teasing by your cynical friends, but let's face it, this trait is very attractive and will attract more positive energy. Your choice, as always.

Adopt a daily mantra of thank you. Thank the bus driver, the waitress, the mail-carrier, the flight-attendant, the pilot. Thank your teachers, doctors, store clerks, co-workers. Be grateful for the food you eat, the clothes you wear, the bed you sleep in. Appreciate your family. Acknowledge the miracle of your body to seek balance. Thank the universe for all the support you get (most of which we aren't even aware of) and for giving you opportunities to grow. Be grateful for your life. And if you find it's too hard to do sometimes, act as if you're grateful. Fake it and feel the resistance that it stirs.

Softening Attitudes *Part I*

If you do nothing else to further your quest for a lighter home and a clearer life, go for this simple technique. Softening Attitudes are a great way to jumpstart the clearing process and will support your journey well after you've cleared away the physical excess in your life. These tools can be especially powerful when you've lost your center and your clearing engine has stalled out.

Here's what they are and what they do:

- The **Attitudes of Being**, aka *Be-Attitudes,* comprise four sets of simple phrases that are meant to soften and erase stuck belief patterns and help to anchor intentions for clearing and letting go. Sets 1 and 2 are introduced in this chapter, while Sets 3 and 4 come later in Chapter 8.
- The **Attitudes of Gratitude** are four statements of thanks intended to help you open up to the infinite abundance of the universe and the

spaciousness of the compassionate heart. The Attitudes of Gratitude place your focus on *having* rather than lacking.

- The *Softening Attitudes* as a total package are not meant to replace your thoughts, but instead ease the stress you hold around your thoughts, beliefs, and emotions, by raising their energetic vibration.

Practicing the Softening Attitudes is like opening up the valve that allows you to release the build-up—the strings and filters—that have been growing unchecked, like mold. Repeating these phrases not only removes the thought mold but also creates an ever-growing spaciousness between the thoughts. The attitudes of being and gratitude can be repeated alternating or separately, ideally with eyes closed, two to three times daily for uninterrupted periods of five to twenty minutes each. They can be practiced with eyes open any time you think of them.

Every person will have his or her own experience with this exercise. For me, several minutes of attitudinal shifting, two to three times a day or whenever I think of it, makes me feel more grounded, sparkly, and spacious. I feel less gummed up, less smoggy, less congested (truly, my nasal passages actually open up!). On days that I skip this simple meditation, I notice a growing tightness and inflexibility around my lower back and knees. I also notice myself getting crankier, my eyes glazing over, and my reserves becoming more depleted. Nothing beats this cosmic lube-job for what it gives me every day with very little effort!

I suggest you practice these every day for at least six weeks if you want to notice an effect, which may still be very subtle. At first, you may have to concentrate a bit to remember the phrases and their order. After a while they will become second nature, like conscious breathing. I also recommend that you re-read the section called "Signposts of Clearing" at the beginning of Chapter 4. Raising the vibration of our belief patterns can bring up some of that troublesome weather.

Note: This practice will help build up your reserves of nonattachment and allow you to feel really clear! If you can only deal with one set of phrases because they're too much to take in all at once, make it the Attitudes of Gratitude. They can change your life.

Be-Attitudes

Set 1	Set 2
I choose ease.	I am enough.
I choose peace.	I have enough.
I choose joy.	There is enough.

Attitudes of Gratitude

Thank ** for my home.
Thank ** for my life.
Thank ** for my body.
Thank ** for my world.

** Fill in with your own concept of the Divine, or your idea of a higher power—which could be anything, or anyone, and can change over time.

Some final points about these Attitudes:

- Handle them as if you would a newborn with all the innocence you can bring. There's a feeling of sacredness to these simple phrases, which came to me through my personal meditation practice.
- Don't be fooled by their simplicity. Each phrase holds a specific energetic frequency and is uniquely powerful.
- Notice which of the Attitudes flow more easily. They seem so simple, but in fact some of these phrases completely elude many of my students. For example, many students find that the "I choose peace" and "I choose joy" phrases from Set 1 are much easier to remember than "I choose ease." For this one, believe it or not, they often draw a complete blank.
- Notice what it feels like in your body as you say just one phrase silently to yourself.
- Notice what goes through your mind (inner critic, what you tell yourself).
- Notice the ones that feel heavier to you or bring up some weather.
- Notice your breathing.

♍ *Try This: Simple Meditation I*

Set up

Alternate one set of Be-Attitudes with one Attitude of Gratitude and repeat silently, twice to three times daily, with eyes closed for five to twenty minutes each time. Repeat anytime with eyes open.

Practice

- ☐ First, find a comfortable place to sit where you won't be interrupted for at least five to twenty minutes.
- ☐ Close your eyes and settle into your chair or cushion and notice the ambient sounds around you. Breathe. Allow.
- ☐ Begin by saying the first phrase of the series. Drop it into your consciousness—like a pebble in a still pond—allowing the mind to do whatever it does. You do not need to coordinate the phrase with your breath.
- ☐ Repeat the same phrase if you wish, or move on the next phrase, as if you were tossing another pebble.
- ☐ Avoid the tendency to move too fast. If the phrases begin to come through like bullets, notice this and slow it down. This is not about seeing how many pebbles you can throw into the water. The idea is to hang out with each phrase in your awareness, one pebble at a time, observing the ripples it creates.
- ☐ Observe thoughts and feelings without managing or controlling these in any way. Allow weather to show up in any of its many forms.
- ☐ Whenever you feel your mind beginning to wander, take it as a clue to repeat another phrase. Seconds or minutes may pass between each phrase.
- ☐ As the mind grows more still and quiet, you may experience longer stretches between each phrase and thought.
- ☐ Repeat the series until five to twenty minutes have passed.
- ☐ Open your eyes.
- ☐ Notice what the world looks like to you now. Do you feel different than you did before you began?

Example 1: Alternating variation [repeats just one Attitude of Gratitude]

I choose ease/
Thank ** for my life/
I choose peace/
Thank ** for my life/
I choose joy/
Thank ** for my life ... and so on.

Example 2: Non-alternating variation

I am enough/
I have enough/
There is enough/
Thank ** for my home/
Thank ** for my life/
Thank ** for my body/
Thank ** for my world/
I am enough/
I have enough …" and so on.

Note: Try to vary the Attitude sets you practice from one session to another.

* * *

Summary: Shift the Focus

- Where the mind goes, energy flows.
- Intention gives the clearing vehicle its direction.
- Your job is to feel what you truly desire and let go of attachment to the outcome.
- Sending out signals of what you resist or do not desire will attract these also.
- Acting "as if" helps you to anchor your deepest yearnings.
- Ritual is a way you can communicate with your unconscious mind.
- Altars offer you a direct connection to spirit and a means to experience your most spacious self.
- Reframing your attitudes is like creating new software; it helps to tame the monkey mind.
- Practicing the Softening Attitudes with your eyes open or closed will raise your energy level, reduce stress, and support new habits of clearing.

② Clearing Practice ②
Refocusing

Goals: The practice this week is intended to help guide the mind purposefully: to realign and amplify your intentions by feeling them, and to notice how by shifting the focus you can change not only how you feel, but who and what you attract into your life.

Reminders: Please remember to take it easy, allow your feelings, honor your limits, and drink more water than usual to offset any possible side-effects of the clearing practice.

Tasks: *Complete the following and add more as time and energy permit:*

1. Every day:
- ❑ Reduce stress and internal weather by following the directions specified in *Try This: Simple Meditation Practice I*. Make sure to vary the sets from day to day and the combinations of Be-ing and Gratitude.

2. Once this week:
- ❑ Feeling Check: Take a moment and notice what it feels like when you repeat these phrases silently to yourself without trying to do or fix anything:
  - ○ "Everything I need is provided for."
  - ○ "Things work out for me without my having to try."
- ❑ Choose one suggestion from the list in *Try These: Playing As If* and notice how you feel.
- ❑ Record in your journal any feelings, shifts, synchronicities, dreams, or ah-has that you notice from practicing this week's tasks and from the clearing journey in general.

3. Optional:
- ❑ Choose one or more rituals detailed in *Try These: Simple Rituals for Clearing and Letting Go* and notice how it feels to introduce these simple practices into your daily routine.

4. End of the week or month:
- ❑ Read Chapter 6 if you feel complete and ready to move forward to the next stage of clearing.

② Clearing Circle ②
Stage Two

Circle Discussion: Complete the following and add more as time and energy permit:

1. Describe highs and lows:
- ❏ Synchronicities, shifts, or ah-has you are experiencing;
- ❏ Any weather patterns that you are noticing as you work with this book.

2. Describe:
- ❏ What it feels like to say: "Everything I need is provided for."
- ❏ (If different) What it feels like to say: "Things work out for me without my having to try."
- ❏ What this means to you: "The universe is a neutral place that responds simply to my focus of attention."

3. Share:
- ❏ How setting an intention makes a difference in your life (e.g., do you always get a place to park if you hold an intention for a spot to open up?).
- ❏ Your personal list of ways to act as if.
- ❏ Your favorite letting go rituals and what it feels like to do them.
- ❏ What it feels like after a closed-eye practice of Softening Attitudes; whether certain Attitudes are more effective than others, or easier to remember.
- ❏ What it feels like to express gratitude; any shifts and openings that you have noticed in your life as a result of expressing gratitude more often.

4. Discuss themes:
- ❏ Use the Summary highlights in this chapter to guide your discussion further (time permitting).

5. Plan next meeting:
- ❏ Logistics, time, and place.

Chapter Six

Put Away Every Day

How we hold the simplest of our tasks
speaks loudly about how we hold life itself.
—Gunilla Norris, *Being Home*

Putting Away As Prayer

When I read the Preface to Gunilla Norris' wonderful little book *Being Home*, I realized that my love of doing repetitive housekeeping tasks, like washing the dishes or putting away the same things in the same places every day, wasn't me just being a hopeless anal-compulsive as I might have believed (and my family might teasingly argue is the case).

Putting away is how I get centered. It connects me to a still place within myself. Folding laundry, or sweeping the floor, or hanging the wash up to dry on a warm and sunny day (and smelling its freshness when I take it down), is how I slow down and quiet the mind. I am soothed and nourished by the ordinary—by what Norris calls "the extraordinary beauty of dailiness." As she puts it:

> "Prayer and housekeeping—they go together. They have always gone together ... In my own life I have found no better way than to value and savor the sacredness of daily living, to rely on repetition, that humdrum rhythm, which heals and steadies. Increasingly it is for me a matter of being willing 'to be in place,' to enter into deeper com-

munion *with* the objects and actions of the day and to allow them to commune *with* me. It is a way to know and to be known … to surrender my isolation by participating in the experience as it happens."[19]

Greta D. Sibley, whose gorgeous photographs accompany Norris' meditations, adds this wisdom in her own Preface:

"If anything we do in this life matters, then everything we do matters. There isn't living and Living. The only difference is how completely we *give* ourselves to living, how we let ourselves be part of the cosmos and be lived. There isn't light and Light, trash and Trash. There is no alternate utopia running parallel to this life. This is it."[20]

Taking care of our things—placing them where they belong when we see them gumming up our lives—can be one of the most powerful, if subtle, forms of bringing our selves and our homes back into balance. In this chapter, you will see how tending the home in small ways gives us an opportunity to connect with our things and visit the spaces that house them. You will see that it doesn't take much to get the energy moving, create new openings in your life, promote mindfulness, and instill a deeper caring for your self, your home, and, the world at large.

No Home, No Have

I have a client who realized that what she needed was easy access to her purse every day, but because it had no "home" she kept tripping over it on her way out the front door. Leaving the house was like navigating a slalom course of purses, keys, coats, and shoes. She admitted that it was an awful way to start the day. This one issue, however, forced her to consider the usefulness of the bookcase that took up prime real estate in the front entrance of her house—smack dab where her purse and car keys would logically go. Moving her beloved books to another, more sensible location, like the study or living area, would require that she displace (or clear) something else to make room for the bookcase. Finding a home for her one little purse started a musical-chair movement of clearing that affected the entire house.

I once saw this staggering statistic in *Newsweek*: "It takes the average American fifty-five minutes every day—roughly twelve weeks a year—looking for things they know they own but can't find."[21] Though I've thought that this outdated factoid (which always seemed a bit exaggerated) could not possibly relate to me, I had to smile when I found myself tearing my entire office apart looking for this very quotation to make my point! I can't say that it took me fifty-five minutes to locate it, but, if I added the time it took me to look for the sales receipt I needed to return a set of curtain rods, plus find the phone number for a subscription I wanted to cancel, I suppose you could say I'm getting up there.

These are the obvious reasons for giving every thing a home, of course. Having a place for everything helps us keep things in order and find them again. It helps us get to the car in the morning without tripping over shoes, backpacks, or purses. Giving things a home also helps us know when we have too much stuff. Finding zero space in the bookcase to jam another paperback, or zero coat hangers to hang the new outfit we just bought on sale, for example, gives us instant feedback that something has to give or something has to go. Housing things properly holds us accountable and keeps us honest.

But, as we have seen already, there is more going on here than the obvious. If we consider the concept of "participatory relationship" that we explored in Chapter 2 and that Gunilla Norris alludes to in her book *Being Home*, there is something vital—something organic and alive—that connects us to our homes and our things. Giving an object that we use and love a dedicated space recognizes its purpose and honors its value to us. Papers, bottles, sticky candy wrappers strewn in the back seat of the car, for example, or homeless CDs scattered helter-skelter, or leftovers molding on the kitchen counter, represent way more than "poor slob" or "hopeless" human behaviors. To me they reflect a level of unconsciousness: a deep disconnect from our environment and our world at large. If you wonder how this can be so, just stop for a moment and use the practice tool we learned in Chapter 4 and *feel what it feels like*—physically and emotionally—to neglect or disrespect your things.

So here's my tough-love position on this issue: No matter how precious, or valuable, or critical your things may be to your personal survival, self-concept, health, or well being, unless you have a permanent and dedicated place to put them, they are ... *clutter!* This means, simply: no home, no have.

Placement Has Its Place

If everything is energy as we learned in Chapter 3, then it's fair to say that the simple act of moving things around will release stagnant energy—no matter what it is. Rounding up a pile on your desk or putting the reading glasses back in their home or simply moving a pile of clutter from one corner to another, gets the energy moving! It is a great way to gather up all the loose ends (strings) of the day. What's more, as we will explore in the next chapter, these practices have the added benefit of creating new neural pathways in the brain. They relax the central nervous system and produce feelings of calm and well-being.

Years ago when I was a teenager, I spent a summer as a Montessori School teacher's assistant for three to five-year olds. Even back then, I was astonished by the level of harmony and peacefulness that prevailed in the classroom. For Maria Montessori the idea of placement was integral to her philosophy, and continues to be a principal teaching tool for developing gross and fine motor skills. Kids as young as two and half years of age learn to respect their space and each other at a very deep level.

In every Montessori classroom, there are cubbies and containers to house every object that a child uses. Things are grouped by function and size: larger blocks together, medium blocks together, and so on. Children can play with anything they like provided they put it back where they found it before moving on to the next toy, game, or activity. Teachers help kids instill these habits by taking their hands and physically guiding them to the appropriate cubby or container, every time until they master the task.

For the Japanese, housing things and putting them away is an essential way of life not only for its practical benefits, but also as a high form of artistic expression. The homes I visited when I was in Japan years ago felt to me like temples; they embodied a simple elegance that was immediately restful and inviting. I was moved by the conscious placement of things: A window framing the garden just so to draw the eye through the interior space in a very restful way; shoes and slippers lined up neatly in the foyer for easy access; futon beds and linens stored during the day behind beautiful *soji* screens to allow a space to serve many uses. The Japanese have much less living space in actual square footage than we do in this country, and still they manage to create a level of spaciousness that far exceeds our own.

The Shaker tradition doesn't hide its useful things behind screens like the Japanese. The chairs, the broom, the tools of daily living—which are beautiful in their own right—are hung right up on the wall in plain view. I can't imagine any American household suspending their coffee pot or blender, but the idea of having one useful thing that is easy to reach and lovely to look at, instead of dozens of specialty things cluttering the countertops, is very appealing.

Imagine what life would be like if we had designated places for all of our things and learned to put things away consistently: putting the receipts away after paying the bills, putting make-up in the basket after using it, putting dirty clothes in the hamper. Takes, what? One second, to toss the shirt in the basket?

So here's what to do:

1. ***Find a home for everything*** even if you still cannot bring yourself to put it away right away like the Montessori kids. Just knowing that something has its own dedicated space helps to quiet some of the chaos. It also feels good when you can put things where they belong, "put things to bed," so to speak. Get yourself a lot of beautiful containers or storage baskets and label them if you have to. This will make your things easy to find later on. If you need help getting started, hire a personal organizer. They are magicians when it comes to optimizing space and creating order out of chaos.

2. ***Give each thing as much breathing room as possible.*** It feels great to put things away into drawers or closets when there is still space left in them. As a squirrel hoarder who used to jam things in so tightly that the closet hinges nearly broke off, this point still feels radical to me. The mere thought of having spaces that remain empty is a huge stretch, and when I am able to pull it off, it feels almost decadent.

3. ***Sort things by kind.*** Place your dishes together with other dishes. Keep all photos together in one place. Dry goods in bulk together. Art projects together. Liquid items together. All coffee supplies together. Socks together in the drawer. Winter clothes together. Fishing equipment. Skis, boots, poles, helmets. Summer clothes together. Big things together, small together. Things you like looking at up front, less pretty things you need in back. You get the idea.

♍ Try These: Moving the Energy

Jumpstarting, cultivating, or maintaining a daily clearing practice requires motivation and a certain degree of locomotion. Here are my favorite ways to create momentum when time and energy are in short supply. They are also terrific ways to promote mindfulness. Choose one or incorporate all four of them into your daily routine:

1. Put away one thing whenever you see it out of place.
2. Put away the same thing in the same place every day.
3. Round up one area for sixty seconds.
4. Make friends with your broom.

Here's how they work:

Putting Away One Thing

Put this book down and take a look at the room you're sitting in. If it's your home or workplace, do a quick scan and see if there is one thing here you are not using right now that is not in its designated home. Now—here's the hardest part (hee hee)—get up and put it where it belongs! If it doesn't have a home, consider the question *why* and the possibility that it, or something else, will have to go. After you have relocated the object, ask yourself these questions: How hard was that, really? What does it feel like to consciously place this thing in its proper place every time? How does the room feel now?

If you're not in your home or workplace, take out your wallet or purse or backpack and do the same thing. Do a quick scan and see if there is one thing in here that is not in its designated home. Set it aside to relocate later, or toss it. Ask yourself the same questions as before.

Putting Away the Same Thing—Same Place

This practice involves putting away the *same* thing every day. Powerfully simple, it will create new pathways in your home, life, and brain! First, choose one thing that you can commit to putting away every day for one week. Choose something that is a stretch but will not elicit stress hormones. Second, find a home for it where it will stay for at least a week. Third, put it away *every day*. After a week of this, notice how it feels. Notice how hard it was. Notice if it has stirred any resistance. Notice if this simple exercise promoted an ease of putting away other things you hadn't planned on addressing. Here are some examples:

- Car keys, reading glasses, remote control, cell phone;
- Coats, clothing, boots;
- Recyclables: newspapers, magazines, junk mail, shopping bags, bottles and cans;
- DVDs in their cases;
- Dirty clothes in the hamper;
- Clean clothes in the closet or drawer;
- Butter in the fridge;
- Crumbs in the trash;
- Car in the garage;
- Book on the nightstand instead of the floor.

Even the *smallest* actions of putting away every day can make a difference in changing the energy. For example:

❑ Lights out.
❑ Turn off the TV or radio.
❑ Put the toilet seat down.
❑ Close drawers all the way.
❑ Push chairs in after eating or working at the desk.
❑ Sharpen the pencils.
❑ Make the bed.
❑ Match shoes with mates.
❑ Close or open the curtains/shades.
❑ Lock the door until you hear the "click."
❑ Push toothpaste tube up and put the toothpaste cap on.
❑ Put away toothbrush, make-up, shaving stuff.

Rounding Up in Sixty Seconds

For one week put everything away in one room before retiring for the night. If it's the family room, pick up the newspapers and place in the recycling bin or the "to read" basket, stack the magazines on the coffee table, return dirty dishes to the kitchen, place toys in the toy box, fluff up the pillows and thump the sofa cushions, rewind the videotape, eject the DVD, place tapes or books that need to be returned to the video store or library in their special "out shelf" or "out box," close the TV cabinet, shut the curtains or blinds, turn the light switch off. *Note:* This does *not* mean reading the article in the paper that immediately catches your eye. It does not mean taking the dog out for a quick walk. This does not mean washing the dishes or making a phone call. This does not mean raging at family members who left a huge pile of dirty dishes. This task is simply to pick up the room to the best of your ability in less than one minute.

Make it quick and fun. Get the kids, partners, or roommates to help. Time yourself the first time you do this if you think it takes too long. Can you do this in less than sixty seconds? How does it feel to return to this space the next morning?

Note: If it's too much to do a whole room, *reduce* the round-up perimeter to smaller areas or piles in your home. If it's too easy to do one room, *expand* the round-up perimeter to include other piles or spaces in your home.

Befriending the Broom

If everything so far is still too much to manage, there's always the kitchen broom! The broom is an invaluable tool and our home's best friend. Get yourself a nice broom and keep it in a prominent, handy place. Here are some ways to make friends with it:

- ❑ Sweep with the intention of invoking a fresh start, creating openings in your life, clearing a path to a solution to a problem that has eluded you …
- ❑ Sweep every day as a practice in mindfulness and letting go.
- ❑ Sweep after each clearing session to bring in new energy to the area cleared.
- ❑ Sweep your front steps to bring new energy, *chi,* or life force, through your entrance.
- ❑ Whack your mattress every six months and turn it over.
- ❑ Whack your bedding and hang it out to air.
- ❑ Whack your sofas, chairs, pillows.
- ❑ Reach and clear cobwebs in the ceiling, window frames, curtains, light fixtures.
- ❑ Pretend you're dancing with your beloved or playing the air guitar.
- ❑ Get your profligate family to get off their duffs to help you!

Tolerations

Tolerations are those niggly tasks or projects that never seem to get done. They've been on your to-do list for so long you don't even notice that they bug you anymore. Tolerations become the background noise of your life: the broken speakers, the frayed bedspread, the box of photos that need sorting, the dirty windows, the squeaky seatbelt or cabinet door, the chipped teapot, the missing buttons, the color printer that needs new toner, the front door lock that keeps sticking, the light bulb that has burned out on the back porch, the drip in the faucet, the slow-draining sink …

Tolerations are also those clearing projects we haven't yet addressed, like taking the stuff to Goodwill or having the yard sale, setting up the auction site on e-Bay, calling someone to take away the junk in the garage. Tolerations keep us stuck in a rut and prevent energy from moving more freely.

In addition to the simple action steps detailed earlier, you can address one toleration every day as a surefire way to create momentum, raise the energy, and feel really good! It's also a perfect thing to do when you only have a short bit of time on your hands.

℞ *Try These: Addressing Tolerations*

Begin to look around at all those things you have simply put up with and make an ongoing master list of your tolerations. Once a week, take a look at your list and address at least one of these tasks. Add the easy ones to your daily regime of putting away. Here are some examples:

- ❑ Replace burned-out light bulb, mildewed shower curtain, bath mat, dirty sponges, stained dish towels, filthy cookie sheets, tired pots or pans, tired mattress pad, pillow, or mattress.
- ❑ Clean windows, rugs, curtains, fireplace.
- ❑ Make an appointment for a haircut, dental cleaning, oil change for car, auto recall notice, closet organizer, piano tuner, chimney sweep, house painter.
- ❑ Feed, prune, or water plants; put birdseed in the bird feeder.
- ❑ Clear bulletin board or fridge of expired flyers and coupons, faded photos, useless phone numbers.
- ❑ Oil squeaky door hinge, tighten screw of shower handle, repair broken window.
- ❑ Organize spice rack, consolidate, or clear out duplicates; downsize extra food storage containers and throw out ones with no lid.
- ❑ Replace standard light bulbs with energy efficient ones.
- ❑ Schedule an energy audit for the house and implement recommendations.
- ❑ Sew missing button, hand wash wool sweaters, put away out of season clothes.
- ❑ Clear and organize computer files.
- ❑ Write thank you notes.
- ❑ Complete legal papers: Living Will, refinancing, etc.
- ❑ Open the curtains and shed more light!

* * *

Summary: Put Away Every Day

- No home, no have.
- Giving things a home recognizes their purpose and honors their value.
- Giving things a home and putting them away promotes a sense of calm and well-being.
- Putting away the same thing in the same place creates new neural pathways in the brain that lead to new habits.
- Rounding up one area is a great way to gather all the loose ends (strings) of your day.
- The simple act of sweeping is relaxing and meditative.
- Addressing one toleration every day is a surefire way to get your energy moving, create openings in your life, and feel really good!

③ Clearing Practice ③
Tending

Goals: The practice this week is intended to help promote mindfulness by tending the home: to develop a new respect for things and spaces, and create new habits that ripple out into effortless action of putting away and addressing tolerations.

Reminders: Please remember to take it easy, allow your feelings, honor your limits, and drink more water than usual to offset any possible side-effects of the clearing practice.

Tasks: Complete the following and add more as time and energy permit:

1. **Every day:**
   - ❏ Choose at least one of the four practices detailed in *Try This: Moving the Energy* and have some fun! Try to include any set of Softening Attitudes and repeat with eyes open while practicing these tasks.
   - ❏ Practice any set of Softening Attitudes with eyes closed for five to twenty minutes, two or three times a day.
2. **Once this week:**
   - ❏ Feeling Check: Take a moment and notice what it feels like when you repeat these phrases silently to yourself without trying to do or fix anything:
     - o "I honor and value my things."
     - o "I honor and value my self."
   - ❏ Address one toleration from the list provided, or choose an item from your own on-going list that needs your attention. Notice what it feels like after having completed it.
   - ❏ Record in your journal any feelings, shifts, synchronicities, dreams, or ah-has that you notice from practicing this week's tasks and from the clearing journey in general.
3. **End of the week or month:**
   - ❏ Read Chapter 7 if you feel complete and ready to move forward to the next stage of clearing.

③ Clearing Circle ③
Stage Three

Circle Discussion: Complete the following and add more as time and energy permit:

1. Describe highs and lows:
- ❑ Synchronicities, shifts, or ah-has you are experiencing.
- ❑ Any weather patterns that you are noticing as you work with this book.

2. Describe:
- ❑ What it feels like to say: "I honor and value my things."
- ❑ (If different) What it feels like to say: "I honor and value my self."

3. Share:
- ❑ What it feels like to put away the same thing, round up the same area, or sweep, every day.
- ❑ Resistances that come up for you that make these tasks difficult; thoughts that might feed the resistance.
- ❑ The effects, if any, that have rippled out as a result of these simple practices of putting away.
- ❑ Your own list of tolerations and what it was like to address one of them.

4. Discuss themes:
- ❑ Use the Summary highlights in this chapter to guide your discussion further (time permitting).

5. Plan next meeting:
- ❑ Logistics, time, and place.

Chapter Seven

Go Slow to Go Fast

When you are rushed, vital connections are lost.
—Unknown

Less is More

It was June of 1985 when the twenty-one-year-old mountaineer, Joe Simpson, and his climbing partner, twenty-five-year-old Simon Yates, became the first ever to successfully ascend the twenty-one-thousand-foot Siula Grande west face in the Peruvian Andes. The feat itself, though incredible, is nothing compared to what ensued for these two men as they made their final, grueling descent.

If it wasn't bad enough for Joe Simpson to have broken a leg in three places, then plunge down a crevasse in the middle of the night to the horror of his helpless partner, and negotiate a terrifying exit down a gigantic glacier with a limited length of rope—it is the remarkable journey of a man dragging his broken body for several days and several miles back to base camp, alone, with only one good leg and nothing to eat or drink that is beyond imagining.

What got Simpson through, he says, was setting the most precise goals. In the film *Touching the Void*,[22] he describes how his mind directed him to move by way of simple dispassionate commands: "Go from here to the edge of that rock in twenty minutes." "Get from here to the edge of that crevasse in fifteen minutes." He would set the timer on his watch and literally, like a rag doll flopping on its belly, drag himself across the inhospitable maze of high altitude glaciers and boulders to his next stop. It would take him hours to cover a few hundred feet. He says that if he had considered the sheer enormity of the task to survive, he could never have done it. Nearly delirious—having lost one third of his total body weight—he managed in the end to meet up with his incredulous partner and lived to tell the story.

If Joe Simpson had not been able to reduce his task into smaller, manageable steps that his mind could handle, he would not have survived. Setting doable tasks and sticking with them, no matter how small they seem in the bigger scheme, is the name of the game of clearing, too.

In this chapter, we will see how, by keeping our focus on "small," and by setting our mind on "doable," we *can* make progress at anything we desire. Giving ourselves credit for small achievements can also make a world of difference in how we experience success. James Redfield in his workbook, *The Celestine Prophecy: An Experiential Guide,* gives us an insight into how we might benefit by acknowledging ourselves in this way:

> "Every time you feel empowered, you exist at a higher vibration. Acknowledge any small steps that you take successfully. At this new level of energy, you will feel as though you are attaining your destiny. This feeling will attract more coincidences."[23]

Clearing with Action

If intention (see Chapter 5) is what steers the clearing vehicle, action is what gives it gas. We can have all the intention in the world, but if we don't back it up with some level of modest movement, we won't get very far. As Will Rogers once said, "Even if you're on the right track, you'll get run over if you just sit there."

It is important to remember that action, as it relates to clearing in this book, is not simply about "doing" something to rid the home of excess. Clearing with action is not necessarily a means to an end, like taking out the trash, or taking stuff to the Goodwill, or having a yard sale. As we have learned and will continue to explore, there is a powerful action in repetition, in practice, in mindfulness, in surrender. The simple practices of putting away, rounding up, and addressing tolerations, described in the previous chapter for example, may not constitute "clearing" per se, but they are terrific action steps that are sure to get the energy moving in your home and life.

For those of you who find the idea of taking baby steps unsatisfying or even excruciating, you may be glad to know that there is an important reason for this. It's called the human brain. In this chapter, you will learn that we cannot possibly create a clearing habit that is both sustaining and sustainable without taking into account the role of the fight-or-flight response.

Fight or Flight

In his wonderful little book, *One Small Step Can Change Your Life: The Kaizen Way,* psychologist Dr. Robert Maurer talks about the part of the brain that governs the fight-or-flight response. According to Maurer, the midbrain is about three hundred million years old and is hard-wired to spring into action whenever we are faced with immediate danger. As he puts it:

> "The fight-or-flight response makes a lot of sense. If a lion is charging at you, the brain does not want you to waste time carefully thinking through the problem. Instead the brain simply shuts down nonessential functions such as digestion, sexual desire, and thought processes, and sends the body directly into action."[24]

The alarm mechanism in the midbrain is called the *amygdala*. It's our body's built-in secret-service agent, if you will, wired to go full-throttle into action the moment it senses danger. The amygdala can be very useful when you find yourself going against traffic on the freeway, or when your (real live) toddler moves towards the sharp knife on the kitchen counter, or when you're trying to survive a hideous mountaineering accident.

The rub with this finely-tuned brain mechanism, however, is that it kicks in *every time* we feel anxious and afraid. The amygdala is not always so useful when you are stepping out of your comfort zone to clear out the letters your boyfriend (whose name you can barely remember) wrote you in high school forty-five years ago, or to clear the *National Geographics* that you have collected since the Second World War.

It's a given that clearing out what no longer serves and supports us will trigger the alarm mechanism from time to time, especially when we are challenged to loosen our grip of attachment. But there is a way to work around this. Dr. Maurer suggests that we can trick the amygdala by taking the tiniest steps as needed to achieve our intended goal:

> "Small, easily achievable goals—such as picking up and storing just one paper clip on a chronically messy desk—let you tiptoe right past the amygdala, keeping it asleep and unable to set off alarm bells. As your small steps continue and your cortex starts working, the brain

begins to create "software" for your desired change, actually laying down new nerve pathways and building new habits."[25]

To bypass the amygdala, Dr. Maurer suggests taking the smallest, sometimes even the most "embarrassingly trivial" steps in the beginning. For the person who wants to cut out caffeine, for example, he might suggest they take one less sip each day. For those who cannot bring themselves to floss their teeth, he suggests flossing just one tooth a day. Overspending? He recommends taking one thing out of the shopping cart before heading to the cash register. In the case of the paper clip, the task could begin by first *imagining* a clear desk for a few days before removing one clip. According to Maurer, this principle applies to any change, "whether the goal is ending a nail-biting habit or learning to say no."[26]

Sounds ridiculous, perhaps, but if there is a simple task or behavior change you wish to bring into your life that has so far eluded you, this slow-drip approach makes sense. It is user-friendly and more importantly, it works.

As we learned in Chapter 2, "neurons that fire together wire together." Adopting a simple repetitive practice creates the neural pathways in the brain that are needed to promote, and support, desired changes in your life. You will find in the long run that snipping off a dead leaf from the plant, or fluffing up the pillows, or sweeping the kitchen floor—*every day*—will create more lasting benefits than if you go on an unconscious binge of clearing the nightmare in your basement. Clearing one small thing at a time with intention is all it takes to soften resistance, get the energy moving, and build the sense of safety needed to clear an entire household. Add gratitude to the mix and you've created a potent formula for change!

Reduce and Repeat (R&R)

For those of you who have battled a lifetime of clutter and find the stress hormones coursing through your body at the mere sight of your piles, I recommend the gentler, "reduce and repeat"(R&R) approach to clearing. It is designed to bypass the fight-or-flight response so that your clearing efforts can last. Remember, baby steps and repetition are the keys to creating new pathways in the brain. Here's how it works:

For every clearing suggestion, *reduce* the time spent on a task, and/or the clearing perimeter, to a manageable size by applying the "rule of one." So, for instance, in Chapter 5 you learned a simple technique to reframe beliefs called the Softening Attitudes. In the daily practice you were invited to repeat the series for five to twenty minutes two or three times a day. That would be the ideal. But for those of you who gagged at the mere idea, I have an *R&R Alternative* of reducing (big time) this task to **one:**

One Attitude
for **one** minute,
once a day,
for **one** week.

When you feel that the practice is a total no-brainer, begin to increase the action by a factor of one each week as you feel more motivated, comfortable, and safe:

Increase to **one** Attitude
for **two** minutes,
once a day,
for **one** week ... or ...

Increase to **one** Attitude
For **one** minute,
twice a day,
for **one** week ... or ...

Increase to **two** Attitudes
for **one** minute,
once a day,
for **one** week.
And so on ...

That's it. Reduce your area of focus to *one thing, one pile,* or *one area,* and clear (or just move) it every day. For some of you it may be the tiniest of steps: just opening one drawer and peeking inside it, once a day, for one week, until you have the courage and energy to actually take out one piece of paper, or one candy wrapper, or one dull pencil nub. The point here is not volume but rather, consistency.

The brain loves questions. You can also keep your brain busy by giving it a simple question to noodle on, like: "What is one way I can clear this office in sixty seconds?" or, "What is one simple thing I can do to support my most spacious self right now?" Trust your higher self to deliver the answer and be sure to *act on it!* Take one small step and repeat it every day until it becomes easy and effortless.

The following examples will help you to practice the slow-drip concept of clearing. The number of repetitions can be easily adjusted up or down. Increase the action when you don't break a sweat anymore and when you are moved to do so:

R&R Method of Clearing the Refrigerator

- Clean, clear, or consolidate **one** item, beginning with the leftovers, moving on to condiments, ending with the stuff in the freezer,
- **Once** a day,
- For **one** week.

R&R Method of Clearing a Desk Drawer

- Clear or move **one** piece of paper, one bill, one ballpoint pen, one paper clip, one rubber band, or just take a peek in the drawer for starters,
- **Once** a day,
- For **one** week.

R&R Method of Clearing Store Catalogs

- Throw away or recycle one store catalog (without peeking inside it!),
- **Once** a day,
- For **one** week.

Addressing Behaviors

If physical clutter is not your thing and clearing it doesn't stir the fight-or-flight response in the least, there is something here for you, too. Perhaps you have a behavior or issue that you would like to change in your life, a weather pattern with which you resonated in Chapter 1. Perhaps you're a compulsive worrier, or a telephone or tabloid or bad news junkie, or someone who is chronically late for appointments; the R&R approach can address these issues, too.

If you're a control freak like me, for instance, who suffers from the need to call the shots, make things perfect, eliminate all margins of error—a condition that afflicts a lot of us first-born children, I might add—this method can help. Maybe you feel totally stale and uncreative. Maybe you're too serious and don't play enough or laugh enough or have enough fun. Maybe you just can't bring yourself to smile at your co-worker, or the cute guy who rides your bus every day. The R&R approach is perfect for any number of behaviors that gum us up.

Be creative. Find some way to apply the rule of one by reducing in small increments the number of times you repeat an undesirable action, or conversely, increasing a desired action by one repetition at a time. Remember to go at a rate that is not threatening and does not kick in the body's fight-or-flight response.

Decrease by telling one less piece of gossip a day. Decrease by reading one less bad news story in the paper each morning. Increase a desired action with one extra smile or allowing one mistake a day. You can change the action when you feel safe and moved to do so. Key again: consistency.

Note: Don't forget to stop and feel! Think of these as wonderful opportunities to notice your weather patterns.

Here are some examples of behaviors or issues to which you can apply the R&R method. Use them to inspire you to come up with your own versions that best fit your needs:

R&R Method to Address Chronic Lateness

- Set the intention to be on time, and actually *be* on time,
- **Once** a day,
- For **one** week.

R&R Method to Address Compulsive Talking

- When you go for the phone or someone's ear, stop yourself,
- **Once** a day,
- For **one** week.

R&R Method to Address Addiction to Surfing the Web (or whatever your thing is)

- When you find yourself logging on, set an alarm clock and log off when the alarm rings,
- **Once** a day,
- For **one** week.
- After a day or two, reduce the time spent by one minute each day or week.

R&R Method to Address Frustrations Towards a Roommate or Family Member Who's a Slob

- When you find yourself ready to rail against your friend, colleague, or loved one, stop yourself and *breathe* for
- One minute,
- **Once** a day,
- For **one** week.
- Try to keep the energy moving by doing one thing for yourself that feels good.

R&R Method of Clearing E-mails

- Delete at least one email that you are saving for no particular reason, without reading it
- **Once** a day,
- For **one** week.

R&R Method to Address Compulsive Perfection

- When you find yourself hyperventilating because something has gone wrong, or, God forbid, you made a mistake, allow the mistake to exist as a fully-formed, perfect expression of imperfection (if that makes any sense),
- **Once** a day,
- For **one** week.
- Increase your practice of embracing **two** mistakes the following week and so on.

Acid Tests for Clearing and Acquiring

When you find yourself not knowing whether something is clutter or not, or in a shop swooning over yet another jacket just like the twenty others you have at home, you can drop into your intuitive self, you can muscle test (see Chapter 4), or you can simply apply the Acid Test for Clearing described here or the Acid Test for Acquiring described after that:

Acid Test for Clearing

1. Do I absolutely love it?
2. Do I genuinely need it?
3. Does it have a permanent home?

Here's what they mean:

Do I absolutely love it?
- Does this thing* lift my spirits?
- Does this thing* make my heart sing?
- Does this thing* serve and support my highest good?
  *You can substitute: room, space, home, relationship, thought, emotion.

Do I genuinely need it?
- When was the last time I used this object?
- Does it have an important and essential function in my home or life?

Does it have a permanent home?
- Does this object have a home with others of its kind?
- Does its home have enough space and breathing room?
- Is this home easy to find and easy to reach?

Acid Test for Acquiring Things

1. Do I absolutely love it?
2. Do I genuinely need it?
3. Where will its permanent home be?
4. What can this replace?

Stay, Go, Throw, Don't Know

As you prepare to clear *one* drawer, pile, or area, here is a simple way to organize your stuff in its current home, on its way to a new home, and on its way out the door:

Four Piles: All the stuff you will be clearing will fall into one of these four main groups or piles:

1. *STAY*
2. *GO*
3. *THROW*
4. *DON'T KNOW*

Sub-piles: When you're ready, and if applicable, each pile can be further subdivided as seen in the chart below:

STAY	GO	THROW	DON'T KNOW
Stays-put *Toleration*	*In-house:* *Transit* *Out:* *Recycle* *Give Away* *Sell*	*Trash*	*Not Sure*

Here's what these piles mean and how they work:

STAY

Stays-put Pile

This pile speaks for itself. This is the stuff that may need a little weeding and fluffing up, but it remains in its current home.

Tolerations Pile

This pile stays put also, but might require some TLC. Tolerations are belongings that you love and use but that need to be repaired, finished, or upgraded (see Chapter 6). They can be set aside in the *STAY* pile or put in their own *Transit* box for servicing later (see below):

- Anything **broken**, chipped, or which has missing parts that can be glued, sewn, nailed, replaced, repaired;

- Anything **unfinished** such as a writing project, a sewing project, a photo project;
- Anything that **needs upgrading** or updating such as electronics, computer technologies, etc.

GO

Transit Pile

This is for all the things that have strayed from their permanent home. I use baskets and hooks near the stair landings to place transit items on their way home. Whenever any thing needs to go upstairs (or down), it goes into the basket. Each member of my family has his or her own basket to temporarily store personal items on their way home. When I'm clearing I might also wear an apron or vest with big pockets for the smaller transit items. Transit items can fall into any of these categories:

- Anything that has a **home outside your home**: library books, the videos and DVDs, the lawn mower you borrowed from your neighbor, the camera you borrowed from a friend, a note to school teacher, materials to photocopy, etc. Place this box or basket of items near the door or near your car where you can see and dispatch it most efficiently.
- Anything that has another **home within your home**: the tax forms on the kitchen table that need to go back to the desk in the study, tools used to repair the kitchen sink that need to return to the basement, stuff from the downstairs that needs to go back upstairs.
- Anything that has another **home within the same room/space**: paid bills on the desk which belong in the file cabinet, clean silver on the dining room table which needs to be returned to the storage box in the closet, wrapping paper on the floor which needs to be put in the box in the closet.
- Any toleration needing to be **serviced or fixed**, which will eventually make its way back to its permanent home.

Recycle Pile

Recycling can give new meaning and life to those things you're ready to let go of. Check out your town or yellow-page listings for recycling options. Each of these recycling sub-piles may require their own special box:

- Anything that can be **reused** or converted into something else: e.g., paper, bottles and cans, rags, tires, sneakers, metals, plastic containers, etc.
- Anything that might be **toxic** and must be disposed of safely: e.g. mercury thermometers, fluorescent bulbs, oil-based paints and paint thinners, car batteries, car oil, etc.
- Anything **large** and unwieldy that can be hauled away and used for parts: junk cars, appliances, tools, electronics, etc.

Give-away Pile

For those things that you believe still have a good "shelf life." Think about those who might enjoy or use what you no longer need or love:

- **Charitable donations**: Clothing, furniture, non-perishable food, Christmas cards to senior homes, paint in good condition, working cell phones for women's shelters, computers, etc.
- **Re-gifting**: Items that you know will be appreciated by friends or family members.
- **Kids' stuff**: Nice, durable toys, books, or clothes, in good condition that your kids have outgrown.

Sell Pile

This is for those things that you would like to **resell**, for example, through:

- Yard sale;
- Online auctions like e-Bay;
- Consignment stores;
- Newspapers, community paper, or Want Advertiser.

THROW

Throw-out Pile

Anything else that has no home in any of the three major piles gets tossed in the trash. This constitutes everything that has no life left to it and has no other place to go. Ideally this will be the smallest of your piles. Some obvious throw-outs:

- Moldy food or condiments from the refrigerator;
- Food in pantry that has passed its expiration date;

- Medicines that have past their expiration date;
- Anything broken that cannot be recycled for scrap (see above).

DON'T KNOW

Not Sure Pile

For anything that is a dilemma: that is, you don't know if it's a *STAY*, *GO*, or *THROW*, you can allow yourself a short period of time to deliberate. (*Underscore*: a short period of time!) If after a few days of deliberating you still feel stuck, you can follow the suggestion in *Try This: Addressing Dilemmas* described later in this chapter.

♍ Try This: Clearing One Area of Clutter

Here are your simple guidelines for clearing one area of clutter:

Your Five Basic Steps

1. **Identify** one area to clear and maintain strict boundaries, like police cordoning off a crime scene.
2. **Gather and label** some boxes or baskets, and have a trash barrel on hand.
3. **Sort** the stuff into the four main piles first, sub-piles second (see chart).
4. **Clear** by using the Acid Test for Clearing described earlier in this chapter.
5. **Put Away** all items that you are keeping in their old and new homes.

Your Refining Steps

- ❑ **The goal** is to have the space that you have delineated completely clear of everything but the items that belong in *STAY*.
- ❑ **Follow a sequence** that begins with *THROW* and ends with *STAY*.
- ❑ **Begin** by laying out all the objects to be cleared on the floor, bed, table, or empty surface in front of you where you can see and work with them.
- ❑ **Sort the stuff** swiftly and efficiently, like a card dealer at a casino. Resist the temptation to linger over sentimental items and things you haven't

seen in a while. If you must connect with a former treasure, set it aside for later so you don't lose your focus.

❑ **Group piles** and sub-piles by function, and size. Avoid over-grouping.

❑ **Move stuff** out of the house as soon as possible. Keeping it in the car or garage doesn't count!

❑ **Reflect** on your progress: notice what went where, how hard or easy it was, what feels different, and how you feel right now.

❑ **Reward** yourself with an activity or experience that makes your heart sing (e.g., a hot bath, a wonderful meal, a cup of tea, a walk). This is very important, as it will help you change your wiring from clutter clearing as pain, to clutter clearing as pleasure.

Your Steps to Success

❑ **Start small and keep it simple** so as not to trigger the fight-or-flight response.

❑ **Clear only** from your selected perimeter. Reduce the perimeter size if you discover that you've taken on more than you can handle.

❑ **Stop and feel** at regular intervals. Ask yourself these questions often: How am I feeling right now? What's going through the mind? What sensations am I experiencing in my body? Is there any emotional weather moving through me right now? How's my breathing? Am I thirsty? What would be the best way to take care of myself right now?

❑ **Exercise self-care** any time you feel overwhelmed, tired, cranky, spacey, nauseous, fearful, jangled, off your center ... whatever. Take a short break. Drink some water. Get some fresh air. Return when you feel ready again. If you don't go back to clearing right away, notice and ask yourself why.

❑ **Notice the triggers** that are likely to derail you. You can work with any resisting behaviors by applying the R&R technique described earlier in this chapter, or by picking up the broom and sweeping your way back to the Four Pile starting point.

❑ **Express gratitude** for all the objects that have served and supported you. Release them with love and appreciation.

▪ *The R&R Alternative of Clearing One Area of Clutter:* Set a timer for a short period of time and stop when the bell rings. Repeat once a day for a week. Follow the Steps to Success listed above.

♍ *Try This: Addressing Dilemmas*

If after applying the Acid Tests you still find yourself unable to move your *DON'T KNOW* items into a *STAY, GO,* or *THROW* pile, you can take this next step, which I call the Short Term Seal-Up. It is a simple technique inspired by author and teacher Karen Kingston.

Here's how it works:

- ❏ Put items in question into a box and seal it tightly with mailing tape.
- ❏ Label the box with a date three to six months from when you sealed it.
- ❏ Put a corresponding note into your datebook reminding you to open the box on the date you have set.
- ❏ Invite a friend (who has no attachment to the contents of this box) to assist you in its unveiling on the date you have specified.
- ❏ Before opening the box, write down on a sheet of paper the items that you can remember storing inside.
- ❏ Whatever you remember is yours to keep. The rest goes into the Recycle, Give Away, Sell boxes, or the Trash.
- ❏ Your friend helps insure you do not peek or cheat!
- ❏ In short, if you can't remember, it's no longer a member!

* * *

Summary: Go Slow To Go Fast

- ▪ Your small efforts applied consistently over time can lead to big changes.
- ▪ The rule of thumb is the "rule of one."
- ▪ The fear response is useful to address immediate danger, not so useful when stepping out of your comfort zone to clear your stuff.
- ▪ The "reduce and repeat" (R&R) method involves reducing a clearing perimeter and/or time spent on a task to a manageable size and repeating the same or a similar task.
- ▪ The R&R method helps you bypass the fear response.
- ▪ The R&R method can also be used to address behaviors or issues that cause imbalance and stress.
- ▪ Every time you feel overwhelmed, reduce the task.
- ▪ Every time you feel overwhelmed, stop and feel.

④ Clearing Practice ④
Easing

Goals: The practice this week is intended to help you reduce the "noise" level in your home and life by simplifying and slowing down; to overcome resistances and get the energy moving by consistently clearing at least one thing, one pile, one area, or one issue, every day.

Reminders: Please remember to take it easy, allow your feelings, honor your limits, and drink more water than usual to offset any possible side-effects of the clearing practice.

Tasks: Complete the following and add more as time and energy permit:

1. Every day:
- ❏ Set aside at least five minutes and follow the directions specified in *Try This: Clearing One Area of Clutter.* If physical clutter is not a problem for you, choose a behavior or an issue with which you'd like to change your relationship, and apply the R&R method.
- ❏ Optional: Address both of the above, one area of physical clutter and one issue or behavior.
- ❏ Practice any set of Softening Attitudes with eyes closed for ten to twenty minutes, two or three times a day.

2. Once this week:
- ❏ Feeling Check: Take a moment and notice what it feels like when you repeat this phrase silently to yourself without trying to do or fix anything:
  - o "When I am rushed, vital connections are lost."
- ❏ Record in your journal any feelings, shifts, synchronicities, dreams, or ah-has that you notice from practicing this week's tasks and from the clearing journey in general.

3. End of the week or month:
- ❏ Read Chapter 8 if you feel complete and ready to move forward to the next stage of clearing.

④ Clearing Circle ④
Stage Four

Circle Discussion: *Complete the following and add more as time and energy permit:*

1. Describe highs and lows:
❑ Synchronicities, shifts, or ah-has you are experiencing.
❑ Any weather patterns that you are noticing as you work with this book.

2. Describe:
❑ What it feels like to say: "I can accomplish just as much by slowing down."
❑ What it feels like to say: "When I am rushed, vital connections are lost."

3. Share:
❑ How clearing one thing or one area, consistently, is making a difference in how you relate to clutter and clearing;
❑ What it feels like to clear one area at a time using the Four Piles method for organizing and the Acid Test for clearing;
❑ What it feels like to address one behavior or issue applying the R&R method;
❑ Which clearing tasks are likely to trigger your fight-or-flight response;
❑ The effects, if any, that have rippled out as a result of the slow-drip practices in clearing;
❑ How practicing the Softening Attitudes with eyes open or closed is helping to reduce stress.

4. Discuss themes:
❑ Use the Summary highlights in this chapter to guide your discussion further (time permitting).

5. Plan next meeting:
❑ Logistics, time, and place.

♋

Chapter Eight

Be the Observer

Leave everything as it is in fundamental simplicity,
and clarity will arise by itself.
Only by doing nothing will you do all there is to be done.
—Teachings of Khyntse Rinpoche

To React or Respond

I have noticed that my emotional storms have not gone away entirely after nearly ten years of active clearing, but they are much shorter in duration. I still have bouts where I'll react, sometimes with a dramatic flourish that is so over-the-top that I might even call it pathetic. Though my ego wouldn't admit it, sometimes my reactions feel forced, like trying to jam my foot into an old shoe that no longer fits. In the midst of some grade-five hurricanes I have noticed that there is this strong witnessing part of me now that just watches with great amusement as I blow my stack.

Here's the thing: I have found that if I can allow the intensity, without doing anything to change it, it does pass.

Every moment gives us an opportunity to "be" with whatever shows up, but if a hot button gets pressed without warning, chances are we will contract and react. Lashing out at someone because they have offended us, for example, not only keeps this particular button alive, but it attracts more people and situations (strings) of this kind into our lives.

In the next two chapters, we will explore the *non-doing* side of clearing clutter. Non-Identification and Compassion are pathways that allow us to clear from a much more spacious, less attached place. They give us the means to be, in fact, *bigger than our clutter.*

Clearing with Non-Identification

Clearing with non-identification is about witnessing. It is a guiding principle that teaches us to become the silent observers of our dramas. We don't fix anything, we don't change anything, we don't push anything. We allow fear to be fear, heartbreak to be heartbreak, guilt to be guilt, joy to be joy. We allow things to be just as they are.

Before you go into cold sweats about this accepting business, you must understand that what I refer to as "acceptance" does not mean that we tolerate the intolerable, or that we don't change. It does not mean that we stand in the sidelines with our arms crossed and our noses twitched up in air watching life pass us by without caring about or feeling a thing—quite the opposite, in fact.

Acceptance means that after we have put into motion our intentions and acted upon them responsibly, *we get out of the way* and *detach from the outcome.* We allow change, we don't force it. We feel our feelings completely and fully without owning or personalizing them. We experience weather patterns as information and feedback.

What gives the whole detachment thing its humanity is *Compassion.* Here in the West, where true caring is equated with doing and fixing, there is no harder lesson to be learned than this: *We cannot hold a space of true compassion for another person or place or being, without first detaching from them!*

Non-identification is not mastered overnight. There is no quick crash course on how to unplug. There is no "getting this." This level of equanimity comes with enormous practice, dedication, and mindfulness, over the course of a lifetime.

Being With Pain

Practicing non-identification invites us to shift our focus. By reframing what we perceive as ours, we can begin to change our entire relationship with a particular stress or holding pattern. One concrete example of how this works is how we hold and experience physical pain.

I have used my own body's aches and pains as my private laboratory. Since I started practicing not identifying pain as "my" pain, I have noticed that most garden-variety sensations recede almost as quickly as they come. A muscle spasm in my foot or calf, which has had the effect of bolting me up from the deepest sleep and disabling me with agonizing ferocity, now passes in less than five seconds. Stomach aches and headaches generally pass quickly, too. Using physical sensation to practice detachment—from simple annoyances to unmitigated agony—has been one of my most valuable teachers.

It is important to point out that I didn't get here overnight. Neither am I a glutton for punishment. My threshold for physical pain is pretty low, in fact, and I'll be the first to go after the usual medical protocols for pain relief if they are warranted and advised and I just can't stand it anymore.

What I am suggesting is that the body offers us an incredible opportunity to pay attention and not identify with every little twinge or hiccup that comes down the pike. If you recall what we said in Chapter 3: not every thing we feel is ours. It's the body's way of processing information that it is receiving from the environment all the time. Physical pain is also an indicator that we are resisting the natural free-flow of universal energy, *chi*, or well-being, which is always there and available to us. Pain shows us our blocks.

One of the ways that I practice dis-identifying with the weather patterns in my life is simply to shift how I language my thoughts. When I remember to do it, I'll replace the subject pronoun *"I"* with the demonstrative pronoun *"This."* For instance, "I have a headache," becomes, *"This is* a headache." "I'm afraid of failing" becomes, "This is fear of failure," "I'm sad" becomes, "This is sadness," "I'm furious" becomes, "This is rage," and so on. It may seem rather simplistic, but as one who favors simple solutions, I have found that this tool, combined with a regular diet of Softening Attitudes, is as powerful as any to provide an immediate shift in focus, and relief.

Caution: The practice in being with and detaching from pain does not replace the role of health care professionals to diagnose and treat physical or emotional conditions. It is very important to remember that if at any point any symptom or disturbance persists in your journey, you need to pick up the phone and get help!

♏ *Try This: Detaching*

This is a two-step practice in observing and reframing your emotional weather. Notice if your attention to this level of detail makes a difference in neutralizing the charge you hold around certain people and situations:

❑ Make a list of human qualities that press your buttons. Use your notes from the various Tune In practices in Part I to help you compile a really juicy, "super-charged" list.

- ❑ Begin by placing an index card over your list and scrolling down each word or phrase to reveal one at a time. Say each one silently or out loud to yourself and notice how you feel.
- ❑ Next, repeat the scrolling exercise by adding the prefix "This is" to each word or phrase. Notice if these phrases hold a different charge for you now than they did when you read them the first time. For example, "Starving child," or "Poor, starving child" would be, "*This is a* starving child"; "Fat," or "She's fat," or "God, am I fat!" would be, "This is fat"; "Tailgating maniac," would be, "This is a tailgating," or "This is a tailgater"; "I told you so" would be, "This is 'I told you so,'" and so on.
- ❑ As you go about your day, notice how your internal storms peak and valley (yes, they do ebb if you pay close attention). At the point where they become almost unbearable, be aware of what happens to the energy immediately afterwards. In childbirth this stage is called transition. Notice your own transitions and the creative impulses that are born out of these. Be mindful of your choice to react or respond.

- ▪ *R & R Alternative:* One reframing with "This is," once, every day, for one week. Increase or change the action when you are moved to do so.

Being With Noise

Nowhere has weather been more in my face but in Mexico where my family and I spent six months on a sabbatical leave. Having been raised in Mexico City, I thought that this hiatus in the country of my birth would be like a much-needed, restful vacation. For me it would be going back to the well, reliving my unique childhood, speaking Spanish again, exploring the cobblestone streets of my youth, writing and reflecting, finishing my book … What I didn't expect was the huge amount of sensory overload and emotional baggage that would come with this package deal.

I had created space in my life to explore, all right—explore my resistance, my attachments, my preferences, my fears, my shadow. The sheer noise outside our bedroom window was enough to make anyone go mad, as the tortilla factory across the street clanked out hundreds of fresh tortillas a day, or the construction workers threw rocks the size of suitcases into a flat-bed truck at four o'clock every single morning. It was the three rooftop Scotch Terriers barking at anything that moved down below, the incessant talk radio next door droning on for hours, and the festive firecrackers going off for no apparent reason at all hours of the day or night. These ambient acoustics of my new neighborhood were just the warm-up!

A treasure-trove of fears and control issues got stirred as well. For the first six weeks, I was in such resistance over the chaos that I ended up nearly paralyzed with back pain. My lower back was such that I could barely reach down to tie my shoes. I felt like I was so out of my element. My circuits were fried. I was depressed. I was miserable. What was I thinking? *I chose this??!*

I felt like a fear-junkie going cold turkey in rehab.

On the other hand, I was feeling stuff that I had never felt before. There was nothing I could do and there was nowhere to go. I had made my choice to go to Mexico for six months, and I had to live with the outcome, such as it was. I had enough presence of mind to know that what I was going through, yet again, was another visit to that dark place I call not knowing. More shedding of stuff.

I sensed something big and transformative was going on, even if I couldn't see past the fears that were spectacular beyond belief. On some deeper level I knew that this nightmare would eventually pass if I could just embrace it.

What came out of my "forty days and forty nights" in the desert country of San Miguel de Allende were some profound insights about the power of the mind: How our beliefs and attitudes create our reality; how pain that we experience in our physical bodies can vaporize in a matter of seconds when we allow ourselves to become completely unattached and spacious. I learned to reduce the mental chaos into smaller, manageable bits, by meditating—a practice I had never cultivated before this point in my life. It was in those bathtub meditations, in fact, where I received the Softening Attitudes that form one of the touchstones of the clearing program in this book.

As Carlos Castaneda reminds us, "We either make ourselves miserable, or we make ourselves strong. The amount of work is the same." After the first few weeks of channeling (and releasing) misery, I came to a new place within myself simply by practicing not identifying with my emotions. Having a really good set of earplugs also helped!

℞ *Try This: Unplugging*

Note: Enter into this exercise with total curiosity. The key is to feel whatever comes up without getting caught up in the mental analysis that it provokes and the emotional drama that it generates. Your concern is not *what* emerges, but *how you process it:*

❑   Close your eyes and think of one thing, event, or person that presses your buttons. Every time you think of it or him/her, it causes a knot in your stomach, an unease that you cannot seem to shake, or feelings of anger, frustration, pain, heartache. Allow your emotions to surface.

If you're pissed, be pissed! If you're sad, be sad. Go for it. Bring it on. Allow. Feel.

❑ After you've had a chance to hang out with this particular charge in your "battery," ask yourself: What is the payoff that I get for keeping this button alive? Allow any answers to bubble up without analyzing them or feeding them with more charge.

❑ Next imagine what it would feel like to let go of your attachment to this issue. Ask yourself: What is the worst thing that would happen to me if I let this go? What would it feel like to just walk away from this weather? Do I really want to let this go? Just breathe in your answers. Allow yourself to feel your feelings without getting lost in them. Be your own silent witness.

❑ If and when you feel ready to let this thing, issue, or relationship go, imagine its grip on you melting away or sloughing off like an old garment that no longer fits. As it falls away, take one step forward out from its grip into a new, more open space.

❑ Feel whatever you feel and keep breathing.

❑ When you feel complete with this witnessing exercise, you can open your eyes and write about this experience in your clearing journal.

❑ Repeat the exercise if you feel that there is still some charge left.

▪ *R & R Alternative:* Think of one person, place, thing, or word that presses your buttons and breathe! Allow your feelings. Repeat for one minute, every day, for one week. Increase or change the action and repeat for another week, continuing until you feel ready to ask yourself the above questions, or until the grip this person, place or thing holds on you loses its charge—whichever comes first.

Four Levels of Awareness

My experiences in Mexico were practice sessions in non-identification. When we can hang out with weather without identifying it as ours, we begin to experience greater degrees of stillness and space between the clouds of thought and emotion. When we stop feeding this weather with our preferences, fears, and agenda, it loses its charge.

Here is a simple tool that you can use to mark and assess your own progress as you learn to unplug. Consider that the journey of self-discovery can be divided into four levels of awareness, where the fourth, and highest level, would indicate mastery.[27] They are:

1. Unconscious Incompetence
2. Conscious Incompetence
3. Conscious Competence
4. Unconscious Competence

To the western mindset, it's difficult to shake off the idea of competency as a measure of something other than "doing." Similarly, the word "unconscious" paired with "competence" at the fourth level can seem like a contradiction. But just to be clear: the model used in this context is intended to illustrate how we humans wake up, incrementally, to our true nature. The four levels indicate a spectrum of human consciousness, where zero awareness marks one end, and pure Presence the other. Think of these levels not as a measure of how well you're doing, but how well you're *be*-ing.

To give you an idea of how this model can be applied to the clearing journey, I offer my colorful Mexican sabbatical as an example:

Unconscious Incompetence would describe my full-blown contracted self: circuits getting fried left and right by the smells, the noise, the disappointments, and the sheer "poor me" overwhelm of my new life in San Miguel. This stage is my "deer in the headlights" reaction to new circumstances that are beyond my control. Because a neural link has been triggered in my brain (see Chapter 2), I'm not at a place where I can even think straight enough to know that I have a choice in the matter. Impulsive, dark, and untenable strategies thrash about in my mind, like pushing the yapping dogs off the roof, throwing a boulder of my own at the workers, or yanking the radio out of its socket. I'm outside my comfort zone; my fight-or-flight response is cranked up to its highest setting.

Though still too rattled to know what the heck to do, Conscious Incompetence would describe me settling down enough to see my experiences for what they are (weather*).* I feel awful. hopeless, and afraid, even though I don't miss life back in the States. Curious paradox. I'm aware of my despair, but have no means to manage or repair it. I try to breathe, sort of. My body experiences localized physical pain, and my instinct is to fix, medicate, and "do" something.

As I begin to embrace the feelings and hang out consciously in this place of not knowing, I enter the stage called Conscious Competence. I'm aware of this period in my life as some sort of journey and do my best to make sense of it. I try not to identify with the back pain and with the fact that I cannot tie my shoes, and getting out of bed kills. The pain thing is my biggest challenge and has a way of slamming me back to level one or two. I notice that when I meditate I feel better. I consciously choose to meditate more. I reframe my thoughts by repeating my new Softening Attitudes like a mantra. I take lots of baths. I notice that I'm very creative these days. I record my insights and I add new ideas to my book that I had never considered before. I read books I've always wanted to read which give me strength, courage, and insight. I ask for help by e-mailing my extended clearing community. I notice more synchronicities in my life. Glimmers of clarity play peek-a-boo with me through the layers of fog. Though painful, my life seems more manageable now and some of the edge, and charge, is gone. My breathing is much better, too—less contracted. I sleep with earplugs.

After about three months I notice that I begin to embrace a lot of weather without my buttons getting pressed as much. With Unconscious Competence I'm able to handle most life circumstances without as much as a flinch. I continue my daily practice in meditation. The dogs bark or not. The radio blares or not. Tortillas clank and go. As I worry less about the outcome, I notice that the four AM rock-tossing occurs much less often, or I don't even hear it. The dogs seem to bark less, too. I feel a sense of quiet stillness prevail regardless of whether there is noise "out there" or not. Feelings come and go. I feel more available and aware. My channels feel clear and I receive some amazing inspiration. I experience a profound opening around my heart which I can only describe as pure yumminess. I'm more in the flow. I feel joy and deep peace and ease. Spaciousness becomes a state of being for some part of the day.

Like a see-saw, I spend the rest of my six-month sabbatical teetering between level three and four with occasional-to-frequent dips back into level two, depending on what the day brings and what I have yet to embrace. This period in my life reminds me of a joke I once heard in Mexico: When tourists ask why dogs bark so much in San Miguel, it is answered with a Zen-like question and an impish smile: Why do you listen?

Softening Attitudes *Part II*

As promised, here are the second two sets of Softening Be-Attitudes. Like the first two sets (introduced in Chapter 5) which support the "doing" side of clearing, Sets 3 and 4 are aligned to support the "non-doing" side of your clearing practice.

To give you an example of how powerful these can be, I found that just repeating Set 3 as I went through severe withdrawal symptoms resulting from eliminating sugar, caffeine, and alcohol from my diet for a couple of weeks, was like a gift offering of manna to my body. At first, I noticed how difficult it was to even repeat some of these phrases silently to myself as they brought up enormous amounts of physical and emotional weather. They showed me how plugged up I was. My resistance seemed to ease the more I repeated these Attitudes. Furthermore, I noticed over time that if I asked my body to *receive* these phrases, the pain I was feeling in my lower back and my legs would sub-side altogether—replaced by an awesome energy of spaciousness that's hard to even describe.

No doubt, each of you will have your own experience with these. See what they do for you. Invite your whole being to receive these phrases by simply add-ing the word "receive," or the phrase "breathe it in," to your Practice. Imagine a thirsty body soaking up the Attitudes like a paper towel soaking in juice, and see if it makes a difference in how you experience them. This daily practice, in conjunction with the other two sets from Chapter 5, will help to build up your reserves of non-attachment, and maybe bring in some higher frequencies to lighten your load. Don't forget to add gratitude, always.

Be-Attitudes Part II

Set 3	Set 4
I am here.	I rest in stillness.
I am now.	I rest in awareness.
I accept.	I rest.
I allow.	

℞ **Try This: Simple Meditation II**

Alternate Sets 3 or 4 of the Be-Attitudes with one Attitude of Gratitude and repeat silently, twice to three times daily, with eyes closed for ten to twenty minutes each time. Repeat with eyes open any time you think of it. Refer to Softening Attitudes *Part I* in Chapter 5 for full detailed instructions.

℞ **Try This: Directed Meditation**

Besides the daily recommended practice described above, you can apply the Be-Attitudes to address a specific issue or circumstance that is weighing you down. Begin first by getting in touch with the weather. Perhaps it's a problem you can't seem to resolve, or a grudge you can't seem to shake, or a feeling of stress and exhaustion that results from something you have no control over, like stay-ing up all night with a sick child, or going through caffeine withdrawal.

Choose a set of Attitudes that best fit the circumstance and practice repeat-ing the set with your eyes closed for ten to twenty minutes, or with eyes open anytime you remember. Notice how you feel afterwards. Is the charge you were holding as strong as it was before? Did you receive any insight or ah-ha you didn't previously have? Notice your body, thoughts, and any additional weather that comes up.

Here are some examples of specific applications of the Softening Be-Attitudes:

❑ If you're feeling harried, rushed, overwhelmed, you might choose Set 1 ("I choose ease," "I choose peace," "I choose joy") or just simply, "I choose ease" by itself.

❑ If you're clearing a closet of sentimental attachments, or taking a box over to the consignment shop, Set 2 ("I am enough," "I have enough," "There is enough") might help you ease the grip and let go.

❑ If you're stuck in traffic, or waiting in line or for a plane that is delayed several hours, or anxiously waiting for a diagnosis from your doctor, you might choose Set 3 ("I am here," "I am now," "I accept," "I allow.")

❑ Set 4 ("I rest in stillness," "I rest in awareness," "I rest") is especially wonderful when you're practicing Yoga or Tai Chi, taking a walk in the woods, or trying to fall to sleep. You could practice this set to clear the channels for added inspiration in writing, music, art.

* * *

Summary: Be the Observer

- Non-identification is pure witnessing.
- Pure witnessing means you don't analyze, personalize, or get lost in any emotional weather patterns.
- Non-identification is a state of being that you cultivate and practice.
- What gives detachment its humanity is called Compassion.
- You cannot hold a space of true compassion for another being without first detaching.
- Detaching makes physical clearing much easier.
- The goal with clearing is to reach the fourth level of mastery called Unconscious Competence.
- At this fourth level of mastery, you allow things to be just as they are.

⑤ Clearing Practice ⑤
Witnessing

Goals: The practice this week is intended to help you step outside the physical, emotional, and mental clutter by witnessing it as that which you are not.

Reminders: Please remember to take it easy, allow your feelings, honor your limits, and drink more water than usual to offset any possible side-effects of the clearing practice.

Tasks: Complete the following and add more as time and energy permit:

1. Every day:
- ❏ Cultivate detachment and release more layers of charge by following the directions specified in *Try This: Detaching.*
- ❏ Support your practice in mindfulness with two new sets of Softening Attitudes outlined in *Try This: Simple Meditation II.* Make sure to vary the sets from day to day and the combinations of Be-ing and Gratitude.

2. Once this week:
- ❏ Feeling Check: Take a moment and notice what it feels like when you repeat these phrases silently to yourself without trying to do or fix anything:
  - o "I am not my story. I am not my drama."
  - o "I am bigger than my clutter."
- ❏ Choose one set of Attitudes of Be-ing and apply it specifically to a situation or weather pattern that needs your attention as described in *Try This: Directed Meditation.* Notice if this practice helps you to detach more easily.
- ❏ Set aside at least thirty minutes and follow the directions specified in *Try This: Unplugging.*
- ❏ Record in your journal any feelings, shifts, synchronicities, dreams, or ah-has that you notice from practicing this week's tasks and from the clearing journey in general.

3. End of the week or month:
- ❏ Read Chapter 9 if you feel complete and ready to move forward to the next stage of clearing.

⑤ Clearing Circle ⑤
Stage Five

Circle Discussion: Complete the following and add more as time and energy permit:

1. **Describe highs and lows:**
   - ❑ Synchronicities, shifts, or ah-has you are experiencing.
   - ❑ Any weather patterns that you are noticing as you work with this book.
2. **Describe:**
   - ❑ What it feels like to say, "I am not my story. I am not my drama."
   - ❑ (If different) What it feels like to say, "I am bigger than my clutter."
3. **Share:**
   - ❑ What it means to "unplug" and how you know that you have succeeded;
   - ❑ A personal "dark night of the soul" experience you have had and how you processed it;
   - ❑ What it's like to revisit your childhood home after years away; the kinds of weather or memory patterns that are likely to surface when you go;
   - ❑ Instances where you have successfully detached from an outcome and what it felt like.
4. **Discuss themes:**
   - ❑ Use the Summary highlights in this chapter to guide your discussion further (time permitting).
5. **Plan next meeting:**
   - ❑ Logistics, time, and place.

♋

Chapter Nine

Choose Joy

You are here to experience outrageous joy.
That is why you are here.
—Abraham, *Ask and It is Given*

Surely Joy

In the town of Concord, Mass., where Henry David Thoreau lived and mused about life, I came across the words by the man himself on a bumper sticker of a beat-up old car: "Surely joy is the condition of life." I stopped and smiled and wrote it down. It has been dancing around in my consciousness ever since.

Surely joy is the condition of life. I swirl it like a glass of fine wine. I smell its bouquet. I imbibe its full-bodied flavors. I savor it slowly like a meal that reveals more of its mystery and perfection with each bite. I swoon over it like pure ambrosia. Hmmm. Can it be so easy?

"Surely joy ... Sounds like someone's name," my husband later remarked over dinner, like "Shirley Joy." I'm thinking, "Yeah, like someone you love to spend time with because she's fun and playful and laughs a lot; she 'gets you' completely, and is totally unconditional with her praise and excitement for you." Shirley is the total opposite of control freak Hilda, whose name I coined years ago to identify that side of me I'm not particularly proud of—Hilda, short for "Hard-On-Yourself-Hilda."

Weigh the two with both palms up: Hmmm, Hilda? Shirley Joy? Which one sounds like someone *you'd* like to hang out with?

The thing about clutter is that it has no sense of humor. It doesn't know a thing about joy. Joy is not within its scope or in its vocabulary. Compared to joy, clutter is one-dimensional. Distracting. Complicated. Dull and flat.

Joy. It is the byproduct of clearing. It is the champagne bubbles of being spacious. It is the natural flow that springs out of clarity. It is the fountain of youth. It is unstoppable, eternal, attractive, magnetic. It is what we vibrate when we are clear.

Joy is who we are.

So if you're thinking, how do I get some—or more—of *that*, let's just say that we've been building up to it slowly since Chapter 4. We've been preparing for this final stage in the clearing journey.

So far we've had the opportunity to experience the first three guiding principles of clearing by focusing our attention, taking action baby steps, and detaching from our dramas. In this chapter, we will explore the fourth and final guiding principle: *Compassion*. Compassion is the softening balm of the clearing process, the part that connects us to our source of pure guidance, supports effortless release, and allows pure joy to simply bubble up.

Clearing without the ability to forgive and be compassionate is like preparing a fantastic meal that you don't get to eat and enjoy.

Clearing with Compassion

Compassion is a clearing pathway that makes us feel safe enough to let go. Held in compassion, feelings of grief or shame, for example, will lose their charge and reorganize naturally into something more spacious, more coherent. Watch a mother hold her disconsolate child without conditions or an agenda or a need to fix or do anything, and you get the idea. The child walks away feeling all better because his mom simply held a space for him.

Really good space clearing practitioners (at the fourth level of Unconscious Competence) are able to clear a space by simply "holding a space" for the home and its occupants. They clear by tuning in and feeling the energetic stress patterns that the client cannot, for many reasons, feel for him or herself. The practitioner can unlock (by feeling) years of trauma (suffering, toxicity, contraction, congestion, pain, etc.) held by the person or place to the extent that s/he is not attached, either to the pattern or the outcome. In effect, it is a practitioners' ability to detach from the weather patterns of their client, essentially becoming bigger than the pattern, which results in its ultimate release.

Compassion, more than anything is a spacious "witnessing presence" that is something we all have. It is the Mother Teresa part in you that sits by your bedside and holds your hand no matter how bad you feel or how awful you look.

It is the part in you that is big enough to feel the worst weather and still not get plugged in by it. It is the part of you that smiles with that permanent twinkle in the eye.

Clearing with compassion is is holding a space for your self.

Expanding Into Spaciousness

This next section is a way to get in touch with what it might feel like to fully inhabit your most spacious self. Though setting aside the skeptic is always a useful practice when we're hanging outside of our comfort zone, receiving the full benefit of the following exercise does not require that you believe in the principles behind it. Again, as always, simply notice any weather that emerges without giving it too much energy and meaning.

The centering meditation described below is based on the premise that the human being is not just the physical body that we can touch and see. Our energy anatomy also comprises a series of invisible layers called "subtle bodies" that radiate out from the physical, much like the growth rings of a tree. If you think of the human body as the yolk of an egg, the subtle layers would constitute the white part—less dense, more of it.

These subtle layers of your energy field contain your entire story: your beliefs and memories, your attachments and fears (remember those strings?), your emotional weather patterns. When these layers are gummed up and cluttered, they radiate out to create an actual, invisible "Pigpen's cloud" we talked about in Chapter 3. These invisible layers form and inform the physical body as we have come to know it.[28]

At the very edge of our energy field is a place I call the Witnessing Presence. It is a place that holds tremendous power because it is the natural part of our energy anatomy that is the most unplugged, detached, and compassionate. If you think about it, it is the edge of your energy field—the eggshell part of your "egg"—that is in direct contact with the infinite and boundary-less sea of information known as the Universal Mind (aka Greater Mind, Sea of Consciousness, Unified Field, God ...). Because of its location in your personal energy field, the Witnessing Presence is the place in your being where you can tap information and receive guidance that is pure, uncontaminated, and limitless. It is here at the edge in fact, where you are able to hang above all the weather patterns of your life. Imagine how much easier it would be to clear clutter from this higher, more expanded place.

If you wondered earlier how it is that a lot of those weather patterns that feel so real to you are not even yours, it is because your big noisy, cluttered field is unconsciously bumping into and overlapping other human energy fields, all the time. Through lack of awareness we each have a way of imposing our big, clunky selves on others. What helps you to maintain your energetic integrity has everything to do with your ability to fully, and consciously, inhabit your most spacious, unplugged self. Expanding your functioning range all the way out to include the Witnessing Presence is like using a muscle you can develop with practice.

The following brief guided visualization will build that muscle. It will help you access and utilize the Witnessing Presence within you, which in turn, will help you clear *anything*.

Make an audiotape using your own voice and practice this visualization often with your eyes closed as a quick way to feel more expanded, vibrant, and less attached! Or learn to laser an abbreviated version in less than thirty seconds and watch the strings and stresses of the world—that are *not yours*, remember—simply bounce off.

♍ *Try This: Centering Meditation*

Note: If you make an audio recording of this visualization, be sure to speak slowly and allow space between each instruction. To help you pace the meditation, I have included a wavy line [~] to indicate a brief pause, three dots [...] to indicate a pause of three to ten seconds or so, and four wavy lines [~~~~] to indicate a longer pause of ten to twenty seconds or more.

Here are a few reminders and guidelines that will help you make the most of this powerful meditation:

- The energy of spaciousness is your birthright. It is free. It is portable. It is attractive and magnetic. It is who you are. Call it in. Use it. Delight in it.
- Know that you can access your own spaciousness, anytime, by simply tapping into the *feeling* of that which makes your heart sing and directing it outwards from the physical to and through the layers of the non-physical.
- You can do this in less than five seconds if you wish by simply activating your special gesture, word, or image.
- The Discerning Field will not keep out what your soul needs to evolve, but it can reduce the amount of unnecessary strings you attract to yourself. The Discerning Field here is not intended as a form of protection as this would imply that there is something "bad out there" we need to protect ourselves against, which only fuels and strengthens the illusion that we are separate (see Chapter 2).

- Practice the visualization anytime you feel contracted, or unsure of yourself, or fearful.
- Practice this visualization before tackling any clearing task.

Find a comfortable and quiet place to sit for a few minutes. Take a deep breath and close your eyes … Breathe out all thought and tension ~ breathe in pure awareness and possibility … Repeat these Softening Attitudes to help you quiet the mind: "I rest in stillness"~ "I rest in awareness"~~~~

When you feel centered, ask your higher self to reveal to you, in ways that you can easily assimilate, what it feels like to fully inhabit your most spacious self … Begin by imagining yourself in one of the most exquisite places on the planet. Imagine it somewhere in nature by the water. You could be on a hill or a mountaintop by a stream ~ or on an empty beach by the ocean ~ or gliding in a rocking chair on a porch overlooking a lake ~ wherever it is, this is a place that makes your heart sing ~ you'll know where to go …

Notice the ambient sounds: the birds ~ the wind ~ the soft cadence of pure, clear, moving water … feel the gentle breezes on your body, their softness on your skin … breathe in the delicate perfume of flowers ~ imbibe their magical bouquet~~~~ Feel yourself dropping even further into state of pure ease, pure peace, pure joy ~ pure spaciousness~~~~

Access the feeling of having enough and being enough. Tap into the infinite abundance of the universe to provide you with exactly what you need when you need it … Allow that you are loved unconditionally ~~~~

Feel yourself embracing the perfect being that you are ~ nothing to fix ~ nothing to improve or prove ~ nothing to change ~ nothing to do ~ this is the energy that springs naturally from the human heart~~~~

Notice your breathing. How does your body feel? Notice any thoughts and emotional weather ~ let it all pass with the breezes …

Now imagine the spaciousness that you feel right now as an energy signature of the most divine perfection ~ unconditional, warm, sparkly ~ a radiant golden glow that can be easily applied and directed anywhere you wish, like a softening balm. Imagine this balm entering your physical body through an opening at the center of your back, behind your heart. Imagine it filling up your "tank," from the tip of your toes to the top of your head. Imagine all your cells, organs, systems, limbs, skin, hair, everything, receiving an infusion of this wonderful, sparkly, soft, golden energy~~~~

When you feel complete, direct this clear, sparkly energy, outwards, beyond your physical body through an opening at center of your chest, around your heart. Beam it out through each layer of your extended energy field: those invisible layers that radiate out from your core like the growth rings of a tree …

Invite this unconditional love and golden light to fill your entire being ~ Feel yourself expanding with each breath ~ all the way to the edge of your field ~ six, eight, ten feet or beyond ~ to the place we call the Witnessing Presence. You will know when you've reached the outer edges of your energy field … Notice what it feels like here ~ to be fully expanded~~~~

Beef up the edge of your field with one more big dose of soft, spacious energy … Ask that it act as a Discerning Field to filter out any pattern or energy that no longer serves and supports you … Experience, by feeling, your most spacious self as a fully-formed state of being that is real and alive …

With a simple gesture, word, or image, anchor this sensation of feeling fully expanded and integrated~~~~

Keep breathing …

Notice what it looks and feels like to inhabit your most spacious self. Are you receiving any guidance or answers to questions you've been having? How does the world look to you from this wider perch? ~~~~

When you feel complete, take a deep breath and bring your awareness back to your expanded self, sitting in your comfortable chair in this room …

Wiggle your fingers and toes and open your eyes.

Stop and feel.

What does the room look like to you right now? How does your body feel right now? What is going through your mind? Notice any weather that might be moving through and allow it.

Growing Pains

The issue of discomfort is so prevalent in the clearing process that it merits another pass. It is so common to experience all kinds of growing pains when the physical body, the densest part of our energetic structure, is the last to get it—the last to hop on board the train being driven by our higher self. Add to this an ego-mind that isn't too comfortable yet with the idea of a change and you might experience an inner tug of war.

Though each person responds differently to clearing, personally, it is not uncommon for me to experience a rash of weather patterns following an extended period of clutter clearing. If I'm paying attention, I'll notice that my body feels very tired, gummy, and congested (like I've just entered a smoke-filled room). My feet often ache. I might experience a few spasms of fear and self-doubt, and my breathing can become shallow. Though it occurs much less for me now, an occasional unsettledness and angst can move in like a low pressure system, and last anywhere from a few minutes to a few days. Mostly I get really thirsty, feel sluggish, and might feel less clear initially, not more.

When we clear at any level, there are periods of expansion followed by periods of contraction. I've learned that these natural ebbs and flows are often part of the package. I've experienced days of extraordinary spaciousness—where I feel like I'm simply gliding blissfully through life in a body that feels no gravity or friction—only to wake up the very next day feeling like I was slugged by a sledge hammer, incapable of moving my neck more than an inch in either direction. Some of my clients might experience these swells after I've spent several hours space-clearing their homes. They can feel so spacious and joyful right after I leave, and one week later be dragging again. To some, it might actually feel worse than before I came.

Before chanting, "This-is-not *wor*-king!" consider what I tell my clients: Clearing stress patterns lifts the lid on the more deeply-held issues that you couldn't even feel before. The fact that you are feeling bad or gummy or congested or immobilized means that you are feeling something! This is good. You are feeling areas in your being that you never allowed yourself to feel in the past. Congratulations—it means you are waking up!

Have you ever held a tight fist for a long period of time and noticed that it becomes numb after a while, and then you don't notice it anymore? When you begin to let go of the grip in your fist, you might not feel much at first and then the hand hurts! Clearing clutter is like that. What you may experience as weather in your nervous system are the pins and needles of waking up after holding on for an entire lifetime! Your job now is to ride the waves with patience and extreme self-care; to remember that feeling "good-bad-whatever"—without attachment—*is clearing!*

Support Equals Real Ease

One of my biggest ah-has in the journey has been this one: It's all well and good to feel our feelings to their full and natural completion, but if we don't feel safe as we clear our clutter, *we will not budge an inch.* What we need is a container that allows us to feel safe enough to let go. In space clearing it is the practitioner who provides the safe container for the client and the space to release holding patterns. In clutter clearing, that container is called self-care.

Think about a time when you allowed yourself to be unconditionally held and supported. How did you feel about life? How did your body feel? How did you feel about money? Your relationships? The future? How did you respond to your world?

My yoga practice[29] is a good example of what can happen when I feel completely supported.

A few times a week I'll lay on the floor and place a number of thick, rolled-up blankets under my knees in order to keep my spine completely flat. Once settled on the floor with this perfect alignment, the muscles in my body, beginning at the tailbone, will soften and relax. After thirty minutes I feel so deliciously spacious, like I do when I've had a deep massage. If I can stay present, the result of such simple support is nothing short of heaven on earth.

Apply the principle of support to any aspect of your life, and you might achieve miraculous levels of spaciousness. In the next section you will learn specific ways to create your own effortless container of support in order to invite release, or, real ease.

♍ *Try These: Softening Poses*

With over ten years of experience with many different yoga traditions, I have to say that the most profound poses for me are the simplest. Some might argue that what I practice on my floor every day is not even yoga at all because the poses I do require so little effort.

For the purposes of clearing clutter, I have adapted two simple poses that require no previous experience and can be done anywhere.[30] The trick is in the set-up. With correct propping and alignment, we allow gravity to do all the opening work for us. Consider these poses when you find yourself waiting at an airport terminal or doctor's office, in your own office, or at home after a very long and stressful day, or when the kids are taking a nap. They go really well in combination with any set of Softening Attitudes presented in Chapters 5 and 8.

Before we begin, read these general guidelines, which apply equally to whichever pose you choose to do. Refer to these guidelines whenever you see these two asterisks **:

- Once you've positioned your body, let go.
- Allow any feelings to bubble up.
- Observe the body—how it holds on and how it lets go.
- Observe the mind—how it holds on and how it wanders.
- Observe the heart space—how the stuff around it clears and creates more space, and yumminess.
- Repeat a set of Softening Attitudes and notice if it makes a difference in the quality of your experience.
- Remain in this pose for as long as you wish.
- Breathe normally.

Chair Pose

- ❑ Sit in a sturdy chair, preferably one with no arms.
- ❑ Make sure that your thighs are parallel to the floor, shins exactly perpendicular. To achieve the right angles if you are tall, place a blanket under your hips; if you are short, place a blanket or two under your feet. (*Note:* Keeping the thighs, legs, and floor at precisely right angles to each other prevents undue stress on the knees, back, and neck.)
- ❑ Place both knees wide apart at shoulder distance, with heels directly under your knees, and feet pointed slightly inwards. Make sure your big toes make firm contact with the floor.
- ❑ Slide your butt all the way back in the chair and place your elbows on your knees. Let your hands dangle freely.
- ❑ Hang your head over like a rag doll, tucking your chin in slightly to allow your neck to lengthen.
- ❑ Allow your head to drop a bit more to create a hollow between your shoulders.
- ❑ Direct your breath along your spine, releasing holding areas.
- ❑ Once positioned, *let go.* Go to ** guidelines above.
- ❑ To come out of this pose, place your hands one at a time on your knees or on the side of the chair. Do not grip your tailbone as this defeats the purpose of the pose.
- ❑ Come up slowly, one vertebrae at a time, with your head last.
- ❑ Allow your body to integrate the effects of the pose by sitting quietly for a few breaths.

Floor Pose

- ❑ On a rug or mat on the floor, roll up three thick blankets so they look like sausages and stack one on top of the other. (*Note:* To create a stable base, fold the bottom two blankets in the shape of a Z, and place a rolled blanket on top of them. Make sure the top blanket is tightly rolled.)
- ❑ Place a few folded blankets, cushions, or stacked blocks to support your feet so they are not dangling in mid air.
- ❑ Lie down on the mat or rug and position the rolled blankets under your knees so that your spine is completely flat on the floor. (*Note:* Keeping the spine flat from the tailbone up releases spinal tension. You may need an additional one or two more Zs and rolled blankets to achieve this.)
- ❑ If your chin sways up, place a small pillow under your head.

- ❑ For greater comfort, you can put a blanket over yourself and place a soft eye cushion over your eyes.
- ❑ Once positioned, let go. Go to ** guidelines above.
- ❑ **Caution:** *To come out of this pose, turn your body over to one side and push yourself up with both arms.*

Floor Pose Variation

- ❑ This is the quickie version of the Floor Pose above; and an acceptable alternative if you don't have the time or enough blankets on hand to set yourself up properly. You will need a chair, sofa, or bed to complete this variation.
- ❑ Lay down on the floor next to a chair, sofa, or bed.
- ❑ Bend both knees and place your legs squarely on the chair, sofa, or bed, insuring that your spine is completely flat on the floor from the tail-bone up.
- ❑ If the chair, sofa, or bed is too high to achieve a flat spine, place a folded blanket or two under your body. If these surfaces are too low, you can raise your legs by placing a folded blanket or two under them.
- ❑ Draw your chin in slightly to lengthen the spine. Place a small pillow under your head if you need one to achieve this.
- ❑ Once positioned, let go. Go to ** guidelines above.
- ❑ **Caution:** *To come out of this pose, turn your body over to one side and push yourself up with both arms.*

Supporting Self-Care

Self-care is like a lotion or a balm that helps us to integrate the clearing. It soothes and smoothes the parts of ourselves that may still feel raw, jangled, and new to the lighter energies of living clear. Self-care helps us to be gentler with ourselves, in ways that honor our process and make us feel nourished and good. It also helps us tap more joy.

Exercising self-care is a daily practice. The "self" part of self-care means precisely that: by *your*self, for *your*self—*not* for your spouse, mother, child, dog, neighbor, best friend …! We cannot possibly be of service to anyone when we are overextended and our circuits are fried. Say yes to self-care and no to anything that does not serve and support you. If your version of Hilda is still too attached to being in control, or needed, you can give yourself a little push by adopting this as your motto for starters—one of my favorite quotations by one of my favorite writers:

"I live by the truth that 'No' is a complete sentence.
I rest as a spiritual act."—Anne Lamott, *O Magazine*

Self-care includes a healthy dose of humor. If you're not laughing every day, it's time to start. Laughter creates powerful chemicals in the brain that act quickly to reduce stress and tension and lower blood pressure. Lightening up your attitude will open new channels and new possibilities for change. It will immediately raise the energy in your home and life and make you feel more alive. The more joy you feel, the more you will radiate lightness and attract lighter people. Joy and laughter is the best beauty treatment I can think of.

I threw a birthday party for myself some years ago where I invited only those friends who would be fun and lively and appreciate Mexican food (my favorite). Instead of presents, I asked my friends to do something that would make me laugh. My next-door neighbor offered his tiny basement theater (yes, believe it or not, equipped with a tiny stage and a state-of-the-art lighting and sound system) for my friends to completely let loose and be the hams they really are. My funniest friend volunteered to act as Master of Ceremonies and was as good as or better than Leno and Letterman. People rose to the occasion and one after the other, outdid themselves. The result was delightful, no holds barred, spontaneous, hysterical, magic! I laughed so hard my stomach muscles hurt for days afterwards. I still look at the video we made of that event and am able to recapture the energy and joy of that moment. It remains one of the most unforgettable experiences of my life.

If you want to support yourself in feeling lighter, start laughing. Laugh with your spouse at the fact that your infant daughter threw up on you twice. Laugh at the fact that your car has broken down for the fifth time. Laugh at the fact that life seems to be giving you one lemon after another. If you can't laugh, try one of those fake, "ha ha" laughs a few times and see what happens. As we saw in Chapter 5, playing "as if" is no different to the unconscious mind from the real thing.

♍ *Try These: Feeling Good*

As the famous poet. Rumi, suggests, "Let yourself be silently drawn by the stronger pull of what you really love." What makes your heart sing? What makes your heart go pitter-pat? What would you choose to be, do, or have, if time and money was no object? Recall what it felt like to fall in love for the first time. What is sure to put a smile on your face? What makes you laugh out loud so hard that your stomach muscles hurt and you nearly fall off the chair?

Here are some suggestions to get your juices flowing:

❑   Make a list of all the things, people, and places that you love. Make a list of experiences that you love or have longed for. Begin to make choices that include some of the items on your list. Surround yourself with at least one thing that you love each day.

❑   Activate your senses every day: cook or bake your favorite dish, buy a bouquet of the most vibrant flowers, listen to fabulous music, install a water fountain in a prominent place, light a stick of incense or diffuse essential oils, place wind chimes on your porch. Clap, dance, rattle, sing—anything to awaken the senses.

❑   Take the time after you've cleared some clutter and honor yourself for it. The unconscious will begin to make the connection that clearing clutter is not only good for you but can feel good too when you introduce nourishing rewards to your clearing program. For example, if it feels good to drink tea out of your grandmother's antique silver set, do it!

❑   Take yourself out on a solo outing or date. This idea was inspired by Julia Cameron's book, *The Artist's Way,* which suggests you spend part of a day—alone—doing something that is total pleasure and connects you to your creative self. Go to a museum, park, library, favorite restaurant, beach, concert, or a show. Do something that you never make time for. Consider that there are some "bennies" to going out alone. When it's just me going to see live theatre, for example, I am often able to get one of the best seats in the house. Make it a practice to take yourself out at least once a month.

❑   Say no to one big "should" at least once this week, and replace it with one big "Yes" that nourishes you instead. Reward yourself for pulling it off.

❑   Practice the Chair Pose or the Floor Pose described earlier in this chapter.

❑   Take a salt and soda bath, or shower, to integrate the clearing work, described in the next section.

❑   "Be with those who help your being"(Rumi, again). Avoid people in your life who aren't cheerful, optimistic, or supportive. Have only the funnest and easiest people over to your home for Thanksgiving or your birthday.

❑   Watch some of your all-time favorite funny movies, television shows, or stand-up comedy routines. Watch "I Love Lucy" re-runs. Remember the one where she and Ethel are stuffing their faces with chocolates in the quality-control assembly line?

- ❑ Explore and lighten up your shadow side with some dark humor.
- ❑ Declare your home a "should-free zone" or a "serious-free zone."
- ❑ Begin your day with this quote from an eleven-year-old boy named Dustin who died of cancer: "Today is a gift. Have fun!"[31]

- **_R & R Alternative:_** Do one small thing for yourself each day that you love and makes heart sing. Pick a flower, smell a rose, hum or sing a melody, take a nap … you know what to do! And laugh once a day, every day, for a week. Fake a laugh if you have to.

♍ *Try This: Salt and Soda Bath or Shower*

This all-purpose remedy will help to mitigate any side-effects associated with clearing clutter. This simple formula was adapted from an old Edgar Cayce remedy by my friend, Bay-area teacher and healer, Desda Zuckerman. She recommends pure, coarse sea salt (instead of Epsom Salt):

- ❑ Use equal parts coarse sea salt (or Kosher) with Arm and Hammer baking soda. It can be a half-cup to a half-cup, or a teaspoon to a teaspoon. It is the ratio, not quantity, of salt to soda that matters here.
- ❑ For a shower, make a paste in your palm and rub it all over your body, including hair, and shower off.
- ❑ For a bath, pour into the tub and soak.

* * *

Summary: Choose Joy

- Joy naturally springs from being spacious.
- The energy of spaciousness is your birthright: it is free, portable, attractive, and magnetic.
- Compassion is not something you do; it is something you are.
- Clearing with compassion is holding a space for your self.
- The Witnessing Presence is a subtle, invisible layer of the human energy anatomy that is bigger than your attachments, bigger than your clutter.
- Expanding your functioning range to include the Witnessing Presence is like using a muscle you can develop with practice.
- If you do not feel safe, you will not let go.
- Self-care is the softening balm of clearing.

- Laughter is a sure-fire way to raise the energy in your home and life; it reduces stress and tension.
- Joy is the best beauty treatment.

⑥ Clearing Practice ⑥
Enjoying

Goals: The practice this week is intended to help you experience yummy spaciousness by nourishing yourself, doing what makes you laugh and have fun, and tuning into what makes your heart sing.

Reminders: Please remember to take it easy, allow your feelings, honor your limits, and drink more water than usual to offset any possible side-effects of the clearing practice.

Tasks: *Complete the following and add more as time and energy permit:*

1. **Every day:**
   - ❑ Flex your spacious muscles by practicing the meditation detailed in *Try This: Centering Meditation.* Use this visualization prior to clearing any clutter this week and/or any time you feel off-center, jangled, or shut down. You can also use this as a warm-up for the Softening Poses or as a cool-down.
   - ❑ Practice the Chair or Floor Poses, following the directions specified in *Try These: Softening Poses.*
   - ❑ Choose at least one of the many ways to practice Supporting Self Care described in *Try These: Feeling Good.*
   - ❑ Laugh at least once. Fake a laugh (not sarcastic) if you have to.
   - ❑ Do something fun.
2. **Once this week:**
   - ❑ Feeling Check: Take a moment and notice what it feels like when you repeat these phrases silently to yourself without trying to do or fix anything:
     - ○ "I deserve to be happy."
     - ○ "Pleasure is my birthright."
   - ❑ Take yourself out on a solo date as described in *Try These: Feeling Good.*
   - ❑ Say no to one big "should," replacing it with one big "yes" that nourishes you instead. Congratulate yourself for pulling it off. Notice what it feels like.
   - ❑ Record in your journal any feelings, shifts, synchronicities, dreams, or ah-has that you notice from practicing this week's tasks and from the clearing journey in general.

3. End of the week or month:

- ❑ Read Chapter 10, the final chapter, if you feel complete and ready to move forward in maintaining a clearing way of life.

⑥ Clearing Circle ⑥
Stage Six

Circle Discussion: Complete the following and add more as time and energy permit:

1. Describe highs and lows:
- ❑ Synchronicities, shifts, or ah-has you are experiencing;
- ❑ Any weather patterns that you are noticing as you work with this book.

2. Describe:
- ❑ What it feels like to say, "I deserve to be happy."
- ❑ (If different) What it feels like to say, "Pleasure is my birthright."

3. Share:
- ❑ What you did this week to nourish and care for yourself; how easy or difficult it was;
- ❑ Reasons you might resist caring for yourself;
- ❑ What it feels like to expand into your most spacious self by practicing the *Centering Meditation*; whether it makes it easier to clear clutter;
- ❑ What it feels like to do the Chair or Floor Pose every day;
- ❑ What it was like to take yourself out on a solo date, what you chose to do and why;
- ❑ List of ways that open you to experiencing pure joy;
- ❑ List of things that make you laugh (e.g., funniest movies, books, jokes).

4. Discuss themes:
- ❑ Use the Summary highlights in this chapter to guide your discussion further (time permitting).

5. Plan next meeting:
- ❑ Logistics, time, and place.

♋

Chapter Ten

Soften Into Spaciousness

This above all: to thine own self be true.
—Shakespeare, *Hamlet*

New *You* Coming Through

There is no telling what will emerge as a result of shedding all those skins of your former self. That is for you to discover as you continue on the clearing path. As the real—bigger—you emerges from behind the veil of stress and stuff, it is likely that you will find yourself feeling and doing things you never felt or did before. Expanding into your natural state of being spacious has a way of making you feel more available and in the flow, as if life were living you instead of you living it.

You may notice that you don't worry as much about the future or what people think as you did before, and your buttons don't get pressed as often by people and events in your life. You may notice that as your attachments begin to lose their charge, your physical clutter becomes less of an issue and simply falls away, effortlessly.

You may experience your body—as I often do when I'm in my "spacious zone"—gliding gracefully through the day, free of friction or resistance, like that feeling you get when you're sitting in one of those glider rocking chairs. You may experience physical changes such as greater ease in movement, a loss of excess weight, a clarity in your eyesight, a softening of your skin … yes, even a clearing of your sinuses!

You may observe longer stretches of quiet stillness between your thoughts, or profound openings of inspiration, or a deep inner knowing that simply takes your breath away. You may notice that the world itself seems more sparkly and alive to you, revealing its divine mystery in tiny details you had never noticed before. Trees shine, people smile, miracles happen. Guess what? This is the world mirroring YOU back to you! Enjoy it. It is just the beginning!

One of my favorite quotations that captures the essence of the clearing journey comes from the legendary twentieth century American dancer and choreographer, Martha Graham. If you've already heard her words, listen to them again with new ears and an open heart; imbibe their wisdom:

> "There is a vitality, a life force, an energy, a quickening that is translated through you into action. And because there is only one of you in all time, this expression is unique. And if you block it, it will never exist through and other medium … the world will not have it. It is not your business to determine how good it is, nor how valuable, not how it compares to other expressions. It is your business to keep it yours, clearly and directly, to keep the channel open."[32]

In this last chapter, we will see how the principles and tools fit together as an organic whole. We will examine how they can be used to create a clearing lifestyle that is both sustaining and sustainable. Once the clearing vehicle is put into motion, supported by a paradigm shift of new attitudes and habits, you can throw away the form and go off-road into the mystery of your deepest, most spacious self!

The Basic Four

As we have learned and practiced, the essence of clearing in this book boils to our ability to:

- Allow, not judge;
- Respond, not react;
- Be more, do less.

What makes this possible are the four guiding principles and foundation for clearing in this book: Intention, Action, Non-identification, and Compassion.

Think of these as equal members of your clearing team that will give you the best possible results. You couldn't do this work effectively without any of them. Consider that action without intention has no rudder, no direction, no purpose. Similarly, intention without action yields only untapped potential. Take away non-identification and you're left with dangling emotional attachments, lots of drama, and a heavy heart. Without compassion, you're unable to get past the machinations of the "toddler" mind; to feel safe, supported, in the flow, and bigger than your clutter. It is worth noting that action, which is the driving force behind most traditional approaches to clearing and organizing in our culture, comprises only one fourth of the clearing work!

Though each principle has been introduced separately in this book and can by itself make a huge difference in clearing your clutter, it isn't until all four are applied and practiced as a *unified whole* that the real magic occurs. It is the confluence of these four energy streams that creates a powerful force for change.

Throughout Part II, we learned that in order to build an effective practice of clearing, we need consistency. In my book, consistency means *daily*. Adopting a daily practice, no matter how miniscule the task or effort, will soften holding patterns and release the build-up of stress and weather over time.

My prescription for a lasting clearing program, thus, is to choose at least one offering from each of the four guiding principles every day. Neglecting one of these pathways would be like taking a leg off a table. The program loses its strength and stability and diminishes the return for effort.

Any time a task feels overwhelming, the secret is to cut back your daily practice by reducing and repeating *all four* elements. Taking the gentler R&R approach means that you reduce a clearing task, perimeter, or time spent on a task to a range that feels manageable, and you repeat the action until the task is complete or it no longer elicits resistance.

Here they are—the Basic Four—your keys to the kingdom of living clear:

1. **Attitudes:** Reframe belief patterns, anchor intentions, and quiet the mind with the Be-Attitudes (Sets 1-4) and the Attitudes of Gratitude with your eyes closed from five to twenty minutes, two or three times a day. Practice with your eyes open any time you think of it.

2. **Action:** Sweep, move, put away, round up, clean, clear, or address *one* thing, pile, area, toleration, and/or issue, every day. Keep tasks small enough to bypass the fear response.

3. **Detachment:** Observe and allow weather patterns by reframing "I" statements with "This" any time you think of it. Repeat silently, "It's not mine," or "Don't go there" any time you feel your buttons getting pressed. Stop and feel often throughout the day—without attachment—to release charge.

4.   *Self-Care*: Create a feeling of safety and joy every day by doing at least one thing that activates your senses, makes your heart sing, and is fun. Practice one Softening Yoga pose every day. Lighten up with laughter.

Note: Keep in mind that statements like "It's not mine," and "Don't go there," are not in any way used or meant to suggest denial. First of all, when you're in denial you don't feel anything at all. Secondly, stress patterns can only be "yours" if you've identified with them. As long as you allow your feelings and weather to circulate freely without adding blame or emotional charge, phrases like "It's not mine" will help you detach with clean integrity. I recommend revisiting the section "Clearing is Feeling" in Chapter 4 if the concept of feeling with detachment continues to elude you.

℞ *Try This: Suggested Weekly Practice*

The Basic Four tools described above provide an excellent base for creating a weekly clearing plan that is easy and adaptable to your needs. The Clearing Plan Worksheet in the Appendix will give you a place to clarify your intentions, write down your goals, track your progress, and hold yourself accountable. You won't need this weekly practice tool after your clearing becomes a natural way of life and you've incorporated the four essential "softening food groups" into your daily diet.

Here's how to use the worksheet to create an on-going clearing practice for yourself:

❑   Photocopy a weekly worksheet from the two-page template provided in the Appendix. If you would like to continue past one week, which is highly recommended, begin by photocopying six double-sided sheets—enough for a six-week period.

❑   Choose one day (preferably the same day) each week to fill out your worksheet. Create a plan that is realistic and doable (*read:* a bit of a stretch, but not overwhelming).

❑   Check off the tasks after you have completed them each day in the chart at the bottom of the worksheet.

❑   At the end of the week, review your progress and tweak your intentions for the upcoming week should you choose to continue.

❑   *Note:* Give yourself a fresh start each week by filling in a new worksheet even if you have not completed all the tasks of the previous week. always praise your efforts no matter how small they may feel. Remember that judging yourself for lack of progress only adds more clutter to your clutter! The worksheet can also be used as a platform to establish and discuss goals with others in a Clearing Circle group described later in this chapter.

♍ *Try This: Suggested Minimum Practice*

Here's a bottom-line practice that will help you begin, jump-start, or maintain a clearing way of life. Try it for at least six weeks and see what happens. Notice any feelings, shifts, synchronicities, dreams, or ah-has you may experience and write them down (see Clearing Journal below). Expand your practice when you feel you can and are moved to do so. Remember to include all four elements in your daily routine:

❑ *Attitudes*: Express gratitude with eyes closed for one minute a day; with eyes open any time you think of it.

❑ *Action*: Put away one thing, every day. The same thing would be even easier.

❑ *Detachment*: Reframe one "I" statement with "This is" (e.g. I am worried = *This is* worry; I have a headache = *This is* a headache).

❑ *Self-Care:* Practice the Chair Pose for at least one minute a day, and do one thing that makes you feel good.

♍ *Try This: Being T.R.U.E.*

This little memory aid will help you clear a path to your TRUE nature. Post it on your mirror, dashboard, fridge, or desktop. Use it as a gentle reminder to incorporate the Basic Four into your daily practice. Use it especially if the Suggested Minimum Practice described above is still too much to manage and wrap your monkey mind around.

• T–Thank
• R–Reduce and Repeat
• U–Unplug
• E–Elevate

The Clearing Journal

Writing down your experiences is one of the best ways I can think of to acknowledge and mark the shifts that are occurring in your life as you clear. What happens when you clear clutter is that the buttons that used to get pressed have a way of vaporizing and you no longer remember what life was like before you began the journey. Think of it as a good type of amnesia that sets in as you progress. By recording your feelings, shifts, synchronicities, dreams, and ah-has, you can see for yourself that things are truly shifting for you—especially if it appears as if nothing has changed! This journal can inspire you to keep going if, or when, you hit resistance along the way. The clearing journal will be your witness, your unconditional friend.

Begin by getting yourself a beautiful, practical, blank book. You'll know it when you see it. This book will become your confidant for a number of weeks or months so buy a book that you love and is durable. Make sure your book is big enough to write in freeform, but not so cludgy that it feels like you're lugging one more thing around.

Your journal is your private record; an uncensored releasing and reflecting of your journey. If you want to feel really safe, I recommend you store it away from wandering eyes.

Write in your journal at least once a week. If you like to record your dreams, which I highly recommend during this time, bring it with you to bed every night. Give each dream a title to help you identify common themes.

After several weeks you may wish to review what you've written in your journal. Use a marker to highlight entries that are particularly poignant and meaningful for you. Your highlights will serve as a quick boost in times when you need the encouragement. They can also be used as your reference notes in Clearing Circle gatherings, should you wish to go that route (see next section).

Remember, the clearing journal will not work for you if you do not work on it.

The Clearing Circle

The Clearing Journal is to the solo traveler what the Clearing Circle is to a group of travelers that share a common clearing vision. The thing that sets the Clearing Circle format apart from clearing alone is the effect of the witnessing process to release holding patterns. The extraordinary power of a real-live human being listening to another—without fixing or doing anything—is the heart of compassion and clutter clearing at its highest level. People often walk away feeling lighter without having lifted a finger to clear at home!

In my clearing workshops and retreats, it is the safe container established at the outset that allows participants to mirror for one another the emotional weather patterns that clutter stirs up. Participants find that their pain or shame, their fear or loneliness, is not unique to them. They see that everyone has their own special brand of holding on: their own embarrassing stories, messy foibles and dramas, silly quirks, dark secrets. These profound realizations help everyone come out of the closet, laugh more, and move forward into that magical spaciousness that surfaces naturally when we speak our truth. Adding other compassionate hearts to the clearing journey increases the visible and invisible layers you are likely to shed, exponentially!

The following guidelines are only suggestions. You may find after one or two meetings that the group will fall into a natural groove which functions more organically than what is offered here. After a while you all will know what works best for your circle.

Here's how to create your own Clearing Circle. The guidelines are divided as follows and described in detail below:

1. Starting a Group
2. Sample Ground Rules
3. Sample First Meeting—Organizing the Circle
4. Sample Follow-up Meetings
5. Secrets to Success

Starting a Group

Think of one to six people with whom you can imagine spending six to twelve weeks exploring your inner landscape. Choose only people that are good listeners and who you trust implicitly. Stay away from any friends or close family members that may make you feel self-conscious or uncomfortable. One way to know is to ask yourself: Can I be completely myself with this person? Would it be OK to cry and laugh and share some of my most embarrassing moments with her/him? Think of this group as a sounding board, a witness, a mirror for you as you begin to peel away the layers.

Choose a person to act as host or hostess, timekeeper, and facilitator for the meeting and rotate this position if it seems appropriate. Set up a time to meet regularly, once a week, once every two weeks, or once a month for a period of six to twelve weeks. After that time, you can evaluate, re-commit, and add more weeks if you wish. If meeting in person is not possible, you can talk on the phone or set up a weekly conference call. Use a headset or speakerphone if you have one. Because the Circle depends on everyone making a commitment to participate, agree to meet for a set period of weeks and decide as a group if there should be a consequence for missing a meeting.

Depending on the size of the group, allow ninety minutes to two hours minimum for each gathering. Kick off with an introductory evening where participants can meet each other, share their intentions, review the ground rules, and receive the first assignment (see Sample First Meeting outlined below). The first assignment could be to buy this book and read Chapters 1-4 prior to the opening gathering.

Note: The six-stage Clearing Practice program is easy to adapt or modify. If it seems like too much for people to read and complete all the tasks that are suggested in one chapter, decide as a group how many sessions will be needed to complete each Practice stage of the program.

Sample Ground Rules

Read this sample list out loud and make sure it resonates with your group. Feel free to make any modifications:

- This is a listening group, not a counseling or advice-giving session; we are not here to fix anything or anyone.
- We are here simply to share our stories of triumph and challenge, and to offer support by listening and not personalizing any weather patterns that may arise.
- In order to hold a space for each other, we will do our best to avoid interrupting and side-talking.
- Everything we say here shall remain confidential.
- We will do our best to speak from our own experience; we will use the first person singular "I" to describe how we feel.
- In order to establish a container that feels safe for everybody, we will attend all meetings, except for extenuating circumstances. [*Note:* It would be good to clarify what those exceptions might be, and if there should be any consequences for multiple absences.]
- Out of respect to everyone in the group, we will arrive and begin on time.
- The person sharing will hold a talking stick or object to indicate that s/he has the floor. Placing the object back in the center of circle will indicate that s/he's finished and someone else is free to speak.
- If no one chooses to speak, we will sit in silence, being mindful of the time allotted for this part of the meeting.
- We will do our best to end on time.
- We will use a watch or timer if necessary to keep the sharing and discussion moving.

Sample First Meeting—Organizing the Circle

Sit in a circle; circles promote listening and healing. If you're the host, or hostess, open the circle with a welcome and, if you wish, an inspiring quotation. Read the list of Sample Ground Rules above, or your group's revised version. You can also read aloud the "Ten Truths About the Journey" and "Ten Keys to Lasting Success" summarized at the end of this chapter.

Once you've established your ground rules and set the tone for your circle, begin with a once-around sharing of the following questions (or some variation) using a talking stick or object. Be mindful that this part of the sharing can bring up some weather:

- Why I am here.
- What clutter represents for me; how it shows up in my life; what it feels like.
- What I hope might happen as a result of being in this group.

Spend most of the first meeting exploring your hopes, fears, challenges, intentions, and remember to honor the ground rules that you have just established.

After everybody has had a turn to share, discuss the logistics for your gatherings. Consider a reasonable time-frame, such as number of weeks, length of session, facilitator, and whether or not to rotate the venue.

Set a date, time, and place for your next meeting, and review the tasks for the gathering (e.g. read Chapters 1-4 and complete Clearing Practice: *Feeling*).

Close the circle with an appreciation, an insight, and/or an inspiring quotation to end on an "up" note. Alternatively, you can conclude with the "Ten Truths" and the "Ten Keys" summarized at the end of Chapter 10, if you haven't read them already.

Sample Follow-up Meetings

Begin with a welcome, an inspiring quotation or an appreciation. Review the ground rules, if necessary. Consider opening the Circle with a set of Softening Attitudes, and/or the Chair Pose, for a few minutes before the first round of sharing. These meditations are great way to help quiet the mind and set a tone.

With the talking object, open the floor for sharing anything that has surfaced in the previous week, or month. Be mindful that side-talking and interrupting can be a sign of nervous chatter (weather). If you are the host-facilitator for this gathering, bring people back gently if this happens.

Allow discussion time in the early weeks to review some of the side-effects of clearing described in "Signposts of Clutter Clearing" (Chapter 4), and "Growing Pains"(Chapter 9). Ask if anyone is experiencing fatigue, moodiness, forgetfulness, mental fog, excessive energy, compulsive behaviors, and so on. You can also discuss the strategies that have worked well to mitigate discomfort, sluggishness, etc. This is an important aspect of the clearing journey; it brings up the opportunity to clear more weather.

After everyone has had a turn, you can either repeat the once-around or open up the circle to discuss the central themes and the questions outlined in each clearing stage.

Conclude by going over your goals and tasks for the week (or month) ahead. Use the two-page Clearing Plan Worksheet (see Appendix) to help focus and manage the task load if it seems appropriate.

Decide on the next meeting date, time and place.

Close the circle with each person sharing one word of how they are feeling in the moment. If you have a little extra time, consider closing a gathering with the Centering Meditation detailed in Chapter 9.

Secrets to Success

To get the most out of your Clearing Circle experience, I invite you to consider these three important points:

1. **Follow the ground rules.** Creating a sacred trust among all the members will insure the most important key to your success: safety. When we feel safe, we are more likely to let go.
2. **Allow silence.** Silence creates openings and opportunities to feel, don't be afraid of it!
3. **Allow the mystery.** Consider this group experience as if you were journeying off-road into the mystery of your own heart. There are no right or wrong answers. No one can predict or know what will happen. Whatever happens is all that can.

An Ongoing Journey: Ten Truths, Ten Keys

In case it hasn't dawned on you yet, here's a little news flash: The clearing journey never ends; it just gets better, more juicy, and more fun!

Because of the nature of this journey to continuously unfold, I invite you to re-visit this book often. You will be a different person every time you read it. You may see something here that didn't register before. You may notice that some of the exercises that once eluded you make more sense to you now. Use this book to tweak and further your practice—to shed the kind of light that delivers those amazing ah-ha moments that make it all worth it. Use it to guide and support you, even as you become more clear! Consider it a safe haven, a pathway to your true self.

That being said, it is good to remember that these practices are only a vehicle. They ultimately do not replace your deeper wisdom to know and act from your own truth. They do not replace your ability to feel for yourself what is alive and cooking in your world. As Lao Tsu so wisely said in 565 BC:

> "Learn to unclutter your mind. Learn to simplify your work. As you rely less and less on knowing just what to do, your work will become more direct and more powerful. You will discover that the quality of your consciousness is more potent than any technique or theory or interpretation. Learn how fruitful the blocked group or individual suddenly becomes when you give up trying to do just the right thing."[33]

Don't forget to have fun while you're at it!

I leave you with two summaries that offer ten truths about the clearing journey and ten keys to your lasting success. Copy and place them where you are likely to see them a lot and allow them to illuminate your path.

Ten Truths about the Journey	Ten Keys to Lasting Success
1. Things change.	1. Keep it simple.
2. Things are not always what they seem.	2. Go slowly, but keep moving.
3. Some things cannot be understood with the rational mind.	3. Honor your limits, be gentle, and do only what feels right.
4. The body knows. Trust it.	4. Let go of attachment to the outcome.
5. Each moment is an opportunity to let go.	5. Be grateful all the time.
6. No task is too small.	6. Be a witness to the weather: observe and listen, stop and feel.
7. Clearing clutter makes room for something new to come into our lives.	7. Notice, and note, what you are attracting—without attachment.
8. Clearing clutter sheds light on that which we have kept in the dark.	8. Invite wonder, not worry, into your life.
9. Spaciousness "in here" translates into spaciousness "out there."	9. Don't take yourself too seriously.
10. It's impossible to fail.	10. Drink lots of water and keep breathing!

Appendix

Clearing Plan Worksheet

WEEK #_____   DATES _____

DAILY PRACTICE—*Choose* **at least one from each** *of the four categories:*

1. *Attitudes* (eyes closed): I will practice the Be-Attitudes Set #_____ and/ or Attitude(s) of Gratitude for _____minutes _____ x a day, every day this week.

2. *Action:* I will (circle one) *sweep, put away, round up, clean, clear, or address the following* (identify one) *thing, pile, area, issue* _____ _____every day this week.

3. *Detachment:* I will consciously reframe "I" statements with *"This is."* I will *Stop and feel* _____ x a day and do my best to allow any weather to surface without taking it personally.

4. *Self-Care:* I will do this _____ _____ to support myself and lighten up. I will practice the Chair Pose and/or the Floor Pose for _____ minutes, once every day.

Continued …

ONCE THIS WEEK—*Fill in as needed and check off when complete:*

_____ 1. *Address Toleration(s):*

_____ 2. *Practice "Centering Meditation"*

_____ 3. *Record Feelings, Shifts, Synchronicities, Dreams, Ah-has*

_____ 4. *Plan for next week* (fill out new worksheet)

_____ 5. *Other*—I will add the following extra clearing tasks or practice(s) this week:

CHART—*Check off each task as it is completed:*

DAILY	MON	TUES	WED	THUR	FRI	SAT	SUN
Attitudes							
Action							
Detachment							
Self-Care							
64 oz. Water							

Resources

Stephanie Bennett Vogt	www.spaceclear.com
Clear Home, Clear Heart	www.clearhomeclearheart.com
Freecycle Network	www.freecycle.org
Master Yoga Foundation	www.masteryoga.org
Masaru Emoto	www.hado.net
Meetup	www.meetup.com
National Association of Professional Organizers	www.napo.net

Acknowledgments

There is no way to explain what it is exactly that keeps people like us hunched over in a bad office chair hour after hour for years on end, breathing life into something that we believe in so profoundly, massaging and molding a vision that doesn't reveal all of itself until the very last edit and re-do, hanging in there when various body parts grow stiff, words don't come, or the bones of a structure you believed to be so solid collapse like little twigs in the breeze. It has to be the legions of visible and invisible helpers that are cosmically and magically aligned to keep us going.

So first and foremost I would like to acknowledge that Divine Order—that Presence—which is always on call and available to guide, support, and witness. I include my own higher "spacious" self here. I am in awe of this amazing aspect in all of us that is way bigger than we even know; infinitely patient with that toddler ego-self that just can't stay still for a second. YOU (big U) take my breath away! Thank you, thank you, thank you.

To those who helped me during the earlier years of this long gestation period: Nina Kimball and Meg Hirshberg, for making the time you didn't have to read my cludgy tome and give me feedback.

To George Vogt, for your artistic insights that helped bring out the best in this book's beautiful cover. To Mim Nelson, Sean LeClaire, Sally Vargas, and Ken Lizotte, for your inspiring tutorials in book publishing. To all the literary agents who took the time to seriously consider my project: your gracious feedback fueled and galvanized me to dig deeper and make this a much better book than I imagined was possible.

A special appreciation to Chris Banfield, for your willingness to edit my work; to take me on, along with all my dangling participles and mixed metaphors. You softened every guillotine blow with the kindest words and comments. Every writer should be so lucky! Thank you also, to the wonderful publishing team at iUniverse, especially Mike Fiedler, Sarie Wilson, and Olive Sullivan, for your honest feedback, editing support, and quick responses to my endless questions! I love how you guys embody a basic tenet of my work: clarity.

To my spirit sister of San Miguel de Allende, Susan Page, for your white-glove thoroughness, gift of time, expertise, and loving support. Your e-mails that encouraged me to never give up were a lifeline!

To my spirit sisters of Concord: Lisa MacDonnell, for reading my entire first draft with such enthusiasm and insight; you helped me see that my book could really make a difference to people on this planet! To Sarah Paino, for stretching me by asking such insightful questions, and Sarah Blodgett for your unwavering support. To Rose Thorne: I treasure the long hours we've spent contemplating the nature of existence between scrumptious bites of chocolate cake and the latest installments of life in the mom track.

To my "third circle" sisters of the Women's Well, for your stories that allowed me to laugh, cry, and hear my own voice for the very first time over a decade ago. As a circle of women doing what women do best, you gave me my first glimpse of what it means to be unconditionally supported, and heard.

To Professor Mary Lombard, my Science consultant and cheerleader. I knew my book was a winner when you took it with you on vacation all the way to the Patagonia!

I wouldn't be where I am without the teachers who expanded my concept of who we truly are and what is possible: First, my deepest gratitude to my parents, Sharon and Jim Bennett, for giving me the childhood that allowed me to grow my wings and fly. I know it was a different era back then, but allowing me to drive a car at fourteen, leave home to study abroad at sixteen, hike alone in the wilderness of Wyoming at nineteen, were some of the ways you gave me the space that honored my spirit. I love you.

To Bambi Richmond, for those amazing metaphysical romps we took as teenagers, with the guidance of your mom, Janey McKim. Who needs drugs when you get to experience the wonders of the mind to do such things like heal at a distance! You checked out too early, my friend, and I'll never forget the gifts you gave me.

Thank you to John Harvey Grey and Chantal D'Arleville for your loving transmissions of Reiki. To Dr. Brugh Joy for offering me a safe passage, through the "gateless gateway" to my deeper self. To Monica Garaycoechea for reminding me that the divine feminine is not something we'll ever "get" with the thinking mind, and for showing me that Her Intelligence is available to all of us humans when we slow down enough to listen. To my Svaroopa Yoga teacher, Melissa Fountain, for the exquisite simplicity and clarity of your teachings. You remind the teacher in me not to take this precious gift I have for granted.

My appreciation to two space clearing trailblazers: Karen Kingston, for choosing me to be among such an elite and extraordinary group of power-houses in the U.S. to certify in a field virtually unknown in the West at the time; and Eric Dowsett, for your help in refining this powerful work to its elegant simplicity. The spiritual subtext of this book is inspired in great measure by your unwavering, brilliant, and elegant message, Eric. Thank you.

To Jean Haner, I honor your unflagging vision, dedication, and support of the "work" that has allowed so many of us to learn, grow, and deepen our understanding of the practice of clearing. I light this special stogie for you, Mummu Mama!

To the Queen Goddess herself, special sister and friend, Desda Zuckerman, for showing us what it means to live BIG, without compromise, and for continually blowing me away with some of the most spectacular glimpses of this mysterious home we call the body.

Finally, to my brilliant and joyful redhead, Cami-B, for teaching me more about lightening up and letting go than any teacher by far. Seeing you blossom with so much self-awareness, humor, and grace, makes being your mom such a privilege and a joy!

And to my best friend and eternal sweetheart, JV, for being my steady rock—my shoreline—during my long dips in this vast (and sometimes choppy) sea of not knowing. Thank you, honey, for sharing this ride of a lifetime that stretches us both and keeps us laughing.

My deepest gratitude and love to you all!

Bibliography

Cameron, Julia. *The Artist's Way: A Spiritual Path to Higher Creativity*. New York: G.P. Putnam, Sons,1992.

Emoto, Masaru. *The Hidden Messages in Water*. Hillsboro Oregon: Beyond Words Publishing, Inc., 2004.

Hicks, Esther and Jerry. *Ask And It is Given: Learning to Manifest Your Desires*. Carlsbad, Calif.: Hay House, Inc., 2004.

Johnson, Robert, A. *Owning Your Own Shadow: Understanding The Dark Side of The Psyche*. New York: HarperCollins Publishers, 1991.

Maurer, Robert, Ph.D. *One Small Step Can Change Your Life: The Kaizen Way*. New York: Workman Publishing, 2004.

McTaggart, Lynne. *The Field: The Quest For the Secret Force Of The Universe*. New York: HarperCollins Publishers Inc., 2002.

Naparstek, Belleruth. *Your Sixth Sense: Activating Your Psychic Potential*. New York: HarperCollins Publishers Inc., 1997.

Norris, Gunilla. *Being Home: A Book of Meditations*. Photographs by Greta D. Sibley. New York: Bell Tower, 1991.

Paul, Marilyn, Ph.D. *It's Hard to Make a Difference When You Can't Find Your Keys: The Seven-Step Path to Becoming Truly Organized*. New York: Viking Compass, 2003.

Pert, Candace, Ph.D. *Molecules of Emotion: Why You Feel the Way You Feel.* New York: Scribner, 1997.

Rilke, Rainer Maria. *Letters to a Young Poet.* Translated by M.D. Herter Norton. New York: W.W. Norton & Company, 1954.

Ruiz, Don Miguel. *The Four Agreements: A Practical Guide to Personal Freedom.* San Rafael, Calif.: Amber-Allen Publishing, Inc., 1997.

Talbot, Michael. *The Holographic Universe.* New York: HarperCollins Publishers, 1991.

Tolle, Eckhart. *The Power of Now.* Novato, Calif.: New World Library, 1999.

Tolle, Eckhart. *Stillness Speaks.* Novato, Calif.: New World Library, and Vancouver, Canada: Namaste Publishing, 2003.

Wilde, Stuart. *Infinite Self: 33 Steps to Reclaiming Your Inner Power.* Carlsbad, Calif.: Hay House, Inc., 1996.

Yogananda, Paramhansa. *Autobiography Of A Yogi.* New York: Philosophical Library, Inc., 1946.

Endnotes

1   Space clearing is an intuitive practice that restores, harmonizes, and balances the flow of energy in spaces at very deep levels. Like *Feng Shui*, space clearing derives from ancient eastern traditions and requires years of training to master. Though the training itself begins with technique, which can vary greatly depending on the tradition on which it is based, it is my view that the best space clearing practitioners rely less on form and more on their ability to hold a space of pure compassion for the home and for the client(s) they are clearing. For information visit www.spaceclear.com.

2   Source: http://www.mcli.dist.maricopa.edu/smc/journey/ref/summary.htm.

3   According to an article printed in an old issue of *Newsweek*, "Home storage products have become a $4.36 billion industry" (June 7, 2004). This statistic is likely to be much higher now.

4   I received this statistic from Dan Pink, bestselling author of *A Whole New Mind*. To learn more go to this link he gave me: http://www.selfstorage.org/pdf/FactSheet.pdf.

5   Described by *Time Magazine* as "A convenient, non-threatening way to connect to other people who share similar interests and live nearby." Source: http://www.meetup.com.

6   I heard this wonderful expression at a lecture given by Lama Surya Das, author of *Awakening the Buddha Within*.

7   I use the term Monkey Mind throughout this book to refer to our incessant mental chatter.

8   I got Frank Joseph's version from http://www.chopra.com/namaste/namaste_feb_27.htm. A slight variation of this verse can be seen on Wikipedia: http://en.wikipedia.org/wiki/Indra's_Net.

9   McTaggart, Lynne. *The Field*, pp. xiii-xiv.

10 *Ibid*, pp. 11-12.

11 Emoto, Dr. Masaru. *The Hidden Messages in Water*, p.39.

12 *Ibid*, p.43.

13 Hicks, Esther, and Jerry Hicks. *Ask and It Is Given: Learning To Manifest Your Desires*, p.15.

14 *Ibid*, p. 61.

15 Rilke, Rainer Maria. *Letters To a Young Poet*, "Letter Four."

16 Naparstek, Belleruth. *Your Sixth Sense*, p. 2.

17 Hicks, Esther, and Jerry Hicks. *Ask and It Is Given*, p. 54.

18 Johnson, Robert A. *Owning Your Own Shadow*, p. 52.

19 Norris, Gunilla. *Being Home*, pp. xi and xiii.

20 *Ibid*, pp. xvii-xviii.

21 *Newsweek*, June 7, 2004, p. 43.

22 This gripping documentary, released in the UK on December 12, 2003, follows the story chronicled in Joe Simpson's book *Touching the Void: The True Story of One Man's Miraculous Survival* which was published in 1988 by Harper and Row.

23 Redfield, James. *The Celestine Prophecy: An Experiential Guide*. New York: Warner Books, Inc., 1995, p.100.

24 Maurer, Robert, Ph.D. *One Small Step Can Change Your Life: The Kaizen Way*, p. 24.

25 *Ibid*, p. 27.

26 *Ibid*, p. 18.

27 The "Conscious Competence" model is used a lot in modern business training and its exact origins are not clear. Several theories are suggested here: http://www.businessballs.com/consciouscompetencelearningmodel.htm#origins.

28 I credit two teachers for giving me this knowledge: To Eric Dowsett for first introducing me to the concept of an expanded energy field that can be cleared using a simple heart-based dowsing practice called "Personal Clearing." And to Desda Zuckerman (who can actually *see* the complex layering and mechanics of the human energy structure) for further expanding my awareness. Thanks to Desda also for the wonderful "egg" metaphor.

29 I practice a very gentle style of yoga called Svaroopa Yoga. Supported poses that utilize a variety of props to achieve specific angles in the body are a Svaroopa hallmark. These poses are specially designed to promote a state of deep relaxation by releasing core tensions, which are said to radiate from tight muscles around the tailbone. The guiding principle "Support Equals Real Ease" that I introduce in this chapter is inspired by the fundamental Svaroopa tenet: "Support Equals Release."

30 The "Chair Pose" and the "Floor Pose" detailed in this chapter are my own adaptations of two Svaroopa Yoga poses. To learn about Svaroopa Yoga,

and/or to find a class in your area, visit Master Yoga Foundation at http://www.masteryoga.org/.

31 I saw this quotation in *Parade* Magazine.

32 Source: http://en.wikipedia.org/wiki/Martha_Graham.

33 As written by John Heider in his book, *The Tao of Leadership: Lao Tzu's Tao Te Ching Adapted for a New Age*, p. 95

978-0-595-41868-8
0-595-41868-6

Printed in the United States
80617LV00006B/98

9 780595 418688